Collins Webster's Easy Learning English Spelling is suitable for everyone who wants to know more about spelling and who wants to write more accurately and impressively. The book uses simple explanations, backed up with examples demonstrating each point, to describe the important features of English spelling. It also points out the most difficult words to spell and offers ways of learning these.

The book begins with a clear explanation of how the letters and groups of letters regularly correspond to certain sounds, and then looks at the reasons why the spelling of some words does not match the sound. Next, it looks at recurring patterns and rules that you need to be familiar with in order to understand and predict how the majority of words are spelled. The last part of the book is concerned with words whose spellings are not easy to predict: it provides some practical advice on learning tricky spellings and then looks at tricky words themselves, showing why each can present pitfalls even to experienced users of English.

All of the hard words that are examined in this book are listed in an alphabetical index at the end of the book. You can use this index both as a resource for checking the correct spellings of tricky words and also to point you to the book's explanations and useful tips for memorizing many of the words.

English spelling can sometimes appear to be a chaotic affair, with the spellings of words such as *choir*, *colonel*, *laugh*, and *yacht* having little relation to the way that the words are pronounced. Yet there are rules and patterns at work in the spelling system, and it is possible to become a good speller by mastering relatively few of these simple rules and patterns. *Collins Webster's Easy Learning English Spelling* is designed to help you with this task, and is a valuable resource for all users of English.

Ian Brookes, 2011

D1344723

contents

contents

the basics of spelling

The basics of spelling

Spelling is the process of using letters to represent a word. For most words there is only one arrangement of letters that is accepted as the correct spelling. Using the correct spelling of a word means that you can be confident of being understood when you write English; getting the spelling wrong can make it difficult to be understood and can create a bad impression.

The alphabet

There are 26 letters that are used to spell words in English:

a b c d e f g h i j k l m n o p q r s t u v w x y z

Each of these letters can also be written as a capital letter. This form is used at the beginning of a sentence or a name, and in certain other places (see page 77–78).

A B C D E F G H I J K L M N O P Q R S T U V W X Y Z

Five of these letters (**A**, **E**, **I**, **O**, **U**) are **vowels**. These are used to represent sounds that are made when your mouth is open.

c*a*t	p*e*n	s*i*t
d*o*g	c*u*p	

The other letters are called **consonants**. These are used to represent sounds that are made by closing your mouth or using your tongue.

*p*ea	*s*ee	*d*o

> The letter **Y** can act as a vowel in some words, such as *sky* and *crypt*.

Most words are spelled using a mixture of vowels and consonants. This is because in most cases we need to open our mouths between pronouncing different consonants. It is not typical to find more than two vowels or two consonants together.

Typical letter-sounds

Most consonants are strongly associated with a particular sound and represent this sound in virtually every word in which they appear. For example, the letter **B** nearly always makes the same sound.

big	*bad*	*bee*
cab	*club*	*robin*

Some consonants can represent different sounds in different words. For example, **C** can have a "hard" sound like a **K**.

cat	*cup*	*panic*

But it can also have a "soft" sound like an **S**.

city	*acid*	*place*

Combinations of consonants

Some consonants can be combined and still keep their typical sounds. The letters **L**, **R**, and **W** can come after some other consonants.

blob	*grip*	*dwell*
clip	*prod*	*twin*

The letter **S** can come before a number of other consonants.

scan	*skip*	*slip*

smell	snip	spin
squid	stop	swim

Some combinations of letters can appear in the middle of a word or at the end of a word, but not at the beginning of a word.

doctor	left	golden
milk	help	belt
lamp	land	ring
tank	went	opt

It is unusual, but not impossible, to have three or more consonant sounds together.

scrap	split	extra

Combinations that produce typical sounds

When some letters are combined with an **H**, they do not keep their own sounds but create a different sound. For example:

CH

chip	chat	rich

PH creates the same sound as the letter **F**.

phone	elephant	graph

SH

ship	bishop	fish

TH

thin	anthem	path

TH can also make a different, slightly softer sound.

    *th*is   *bother*   *see*the

Simple vowel sounds

The vowels **A**, **E**, **I**, **O**, and **U** each have typical sounds when they appear on their own in short words.

cat	*rat*	*hat*
men	*pen*	*ten*
bit	*hit*	*sit*
dot	*lot*	*got*
but	*nut*	*hut*

The sound of a vowel changes from a "short" sound to a "long" sound when the consonant after the vowel is followed by the letter **E**.

date	*rate*	*hate*
scene	*cede*	*theme*
bite	*mite*	*like*
note	*lone*	*mole*
flute	*rule*	*brute*

Combinations of vowels

When two vowels are used together, they usually make a different sound rather than keeping the simple sounds they make on their own.

The letters **AI** have a characteristic sound when they appear together.

    raid   *train*   *aim*

The letters **AU** have a characteristic sound when they appear together.

daub   *faun*   *haul*

The letters **EA** have a characteristic sound when they appear together.

read   *tea*   *eat*

When the letter **E** is doubled it produces a characteristic sound.
The sound is the same as the one typically produced by **EA**.

feed   *tree*   *bee*

The letters **IE** have a characteristic sound when they appear together.

tie   *fried*   *pie*

The letters **OA** have a characteristic sound when they appear together.

road   *goat*   *toad*

The letters **OE** have a characteristic sound when they appear together,
usually at the end of a word. The sound is the same as the one typically
produced by **OA**.

toe   *hoe*   *woe*

The letters **OI** have a characteristic sound when they appear together.

coin   *soil*   *oil*

When the letter **O** is doubled it produces a characteristic sound.

food   *moon*   *boot*

The double **O** can sometimes make a different, shorter, sound.

good   *wool*   *hood*

The letters **OU** have a characteristic sound when they appear together.

    mouth   *count*   *out*

The letters **UE** have a characteristic sound when they appear together. The sound is the same as the one produced by **OO** in the word *food*.

    true   *sue*   *glue*

Vowels followed by R

The letter **R** slightly changes the sound of most single vowels that come before it.

The letters **AR** have a characteristic sound when they appear together.

    car   *park*   *art*

The letters **ER** have a characteristic sound when they appear together.

    her   *term*   *herb*

The letters **IR** have a characteristic sound when they appear together.

    sir   *girl*   *shirt*

The letters **OR** have a characteristic sound when they appear together.

    sort   *born*   *for*

The letters **UR** have a characteristic sound when they appear together. The sound is the same as the one typically produced by **ER**.

    burn   *turn*   *hurt*

Vowels followed by W or Y

When the letters **W** or **Y** come after a vowel, the letter usually changes the sound of the vowel, but it is not sounded itself.

The letters **AW** have a characteristic sound when they appear together at the end of a word or syllable. The sound is the same as the one typically produced by **AU**.

*p**aw***   *cl**aw***   *str**aw***

The letters **AY** have a characteristic sound when they appear together at the end of a word or syllable. The sound is the same as the one typically produced by **AI**.

*d**ay***   *st**ay***   *m**ay***

The letters **EW** have a characteristic sound when they appear together at the end of a word or syllable. The sound is the same as the one produced by **OO** in the word food.

*fl**ew***   *y**ew***   *br**ew***

The letters **OW** have a characteristic sound when they appear together at the end of a word or syllable. The sound is the same as the one typically produced by **OU**.

*h**ow***   *gr**ow**l*   *d**ow**n*

These letters can also make the sound that is typically produced by **OE**.

*gr**ow***   *fl**ow***   ***ow**n*

The letters **OY** have a characteristic sound when they appear together. The sound is the same as the one typically produced by **OI**.

*b**oy***   *t**oy***   *j**oy***

why you need to work at spelling

Why you need to work at spelling

If every letter represented one sound and one sound only, you could write out words very easily once you knew which letter represented which sound. Some languages (such as Italian) are like this, and present few surprises with regard to spelling once you know how each sound is written.

But English uses about 44 different sounds to make up words, whereas there are only 26 letters to indicate these sounds. This means that some letters have to be used for more than one sound.

Moreover, there are certain other factors that mean it is not always easy to predict how an English word will be spelled. We will look at these factors in this chapter.

Some letters can have more than one sound

As we have just seen, there are more sounds in English than there are letters to represent them. This means that some letters have to represent more than one sound.

For example, the letter **T** usually makes the same sound when it occurs on its own.

tin *tank* *pat*

But it makes different sounds when it is followed by **H**.

thin *this* *path*

More awkwardly, some letters have more than one sound, even
though there are other letters that make one of the sounds.
For example, the letter **G** typically has a "hard" sound.

    *g*irl   ti*g*er   ru*g*

But in some cases it makes the same "soft" sound as the letter **J**.

    *g*erm   *g*in*g*er   pa*g*e

Similarly, the letter **S** has a characteristic "hissing" sound.

    *s*ee   *s*it   ga*s*

But it can sometimes make the same "buzzing" sound as the letter **Z**.

    ha*s*   hi*s*   plea*s*ant

The fact that letters can represent multiple sounds means that when
you see a word you cannot automatically know how it will be
pronounced.

Some sounds can be represented by different letters

A more significant issue for spelling is that, because some sounds can
be represented by different letters or combinations of letters, you cannot
automatically know how a word will be spelled when you hear it.

The vowel sound in the following group of words has the same
pronunciation, but the letters used to represent the sound are
different in each word.

    m*ar*ch   *al*ms   bl*ah*   h*ear*t

The same thing can be true of most vowel sounds, as the following groups of words show.

*ai*sle	*gu*y	m*igh*t	r*ye*
p*ai*d	d*ay*	pr*ey*	n*eigh*
b*ea*d	c*e*de	d*ee*d	k*ey*ed
z*oo*	d*o*	sh*oe*	y*ou*

Similarly, the consonant sound at the end of the following words has the same pronunciation, but is represented by different letters in each word.

i*f*	gra*ph*	rou*gh*

The same thing can be true of other consonant sounds, as the following groups of words show.

*g*em	e*dg*e	*j*am
*c*ap	*d*ark	pla*qu*e
*s*it	*c*enter	*sc*ene

So when you hear a word, you can't automatically work out how it is spelled, though you can often make a good guess.

Some words that sound the same are written differently

Because sounds can be represented by different letters, it is possible for two different words to sound the same but be spelled differently. This can lead to confusion between the two spellings.

For example, the words *there*, meaning "that place," and *their*, meaning "belonging to them," both have the same sound. Similarly, the words *stare*, meaning "to look intently," and *stair*, meaning "one of a set of steps," also share a single pronunciation.

It can be easy to confuse these words and use the correct spelling of one word when you are actually intending to write the other word.

English words come from many different languages

One of the most striking features of the English language is its readiness to accept words from other languages. At the heart of modern English are two completely different languages – Anglo-Saxon and French – which have two different spelling systems, but which both contributed thousands of words to English. In addition to this, English has borrowed words from many other European languages, such as Italian, Spanish, German, and Dutch. Furthermore, whenever scientists made new discoveries they turned to the classical languages of Latin and Greek to come up with names for the new things they needed to describe.

As communications between different parts of the world have become easier, more and more languages have contributed to English, including Turkish, Arabic, Hindi, Chinese, Japanese, and Russian.

Each of these languages has its own spelling system – many of which are quite different from the natural English system – and the words that English has borrowed from them often keep the spelling patterns of the original language.

For example, many words that come from French use **CH** where you might expect **SH**.

    *ch*alet   *ch*ute   *ch*auffeur

Words that come from Greek usually use **PH** rather than **F**.

    tele*ph*one   *ph*ysical   *ph*otograph

Words that come from Japanese use **K** rather than **C**.

karaoke   *karate*   *kimono*

So the pronunciation of a word might suggest to you any number of different spellings if you don't know which language the word came from.

Silent letters

Another thing that can be confusing is that some words contain letters that are not sounded when the word is pronounced.

Often these are letters that were sounded in the original form of a word. Over many years the pronunciation of these words became simplified, but the spelling did not change to reflect the new pronunciation.

For example, the letter **G** is often silent before **N** or **M**.

gnat   *phlegm*   *sign*

Similarly, **H** is often silent at the start of a word, or after **G** or **R**.

honest   *ghost*   *rhyme*

E is often silent at the end of words.

have   *give*   *love*

> In fact, it has been reckoned that of the 26 letters in the alphabet, only five are never silent. These five are **F**, **J**, **Q**, **V**, and **X**.

The presence of single and double letters

All of the letters except **H**, **Q**, and **Y** can occur as both single and double letters within a word.

For example, the letter **B** occurs as a single letter in some words.

    *ro*b*in*   *ha*b*it*   *cra*b*

But in other words the **B** is doubled.

    *bo*bb*in*   *ra*bb*it*   *e*bb*

When consonants are doubled, they are pronounced just the same as a single consonant. So when you hear a word you cannot always tell where a consonant sound is represented by a single letter or a double letter.

Spelling variants

Some words do not have a single spelling that is regarded as correct, but can be spelled in two or more different ways.

Some words that come from other languages can be written in different ways in English because the original language uses a different alphabet and there are different systems for representing that alphabet in English.

veranda	*verandah*
czar	*tsar*
alleluia	*hallelujah*

Other spelling variations are simply a matter of taste.

barbecue	*Bar-B-Q*
judgment	*judgement*

The fact that such variations exist means that for some words there is not always a single correct spelling that you can learn.

American and British spelling

One of the most common sources of variations in spelling is the fact that some words are conventionally spelled differently in American English and British English. Some spellings that are regarded as correct by American speakers are not used in Britain (or in Australia and most other English-speaking countries). Canadian English uses spellings that match the American spellings for some words and the British spellings for others.

The table below shows some examples of variations between British and American spelling.

American English	British English
aluminum	aluminium
analyze	analyse
anesthetic	anaesthetic
ax	axe
behavior	behaviour
breathalyze	breathalyse
catalog	catalogue
center	centre
check	cheque
color	colour
curb	kerb
defense	defence
favorite	favourite
fulfill	fulfil
gray	grey
installment	instalment
jewelry	jewellery
liter	litre
luster	lustre

American English	British English
meager	meagre
mold	mould
mustache	moustache
odor	odour
percent	per cent
plow	plough
program	programme
pajamas	pyjamas
skeptic	sceptic
sulfur	sulphur
theater	theatre
tire	tyre

And now the good news

All of these factors mean that English spelling needs some work before you can become very accurate. The good news, however, is that there are things you can do to help you understand the system better and so become confident about how to spell words. We will look at these in the next two chapters.

patterns and building blocks

Patterns and building blocks

Some groups of letters appear in many different English words.
Often a group of letters will indicate the same thing in every word
where it appears. For example, the letters **RE** at the start of a word
usually mean "again."

Because so many words are made up of these building blocks, you
don't need to learn every spelling individually. Often you can spell
out a word by adding together the blocks of letters that form the word.
So it is important to know what these blocks are, how they are joined
to the rest of a word, and what they mean.

Building blocks at the start of words

A block of letters that regularly appears at the start of words and
carries a meaning is called a **prefix**. A prefix can be attached in front of
another word or block of letters to create a new word with a different
meaning.

For example, when the letters **UN** are added to another word
(called a **root word**), they add the meaning of "not" to the sense of
the other word.

*un*natural   *un*known   *un*holy

Notice that you can spell these words by splitting them into the prefix
and the root word, as the spelling of the root word stays the same.

It is not always so obvious that a prefix is being added to an existing
word to make a new word. Many prefixes occur in words that came to
English from Latin and Greek. In these cases the blocks to which they
are joined are often Latin or Greek forms rather than familiar English
words. Nevertheless, it is worth studying these building blocks and
noting that they occur in many English words.

The prefix **AB** means "away from" or "not."

    *ab*normal   *ab*use   *ab*scond

The prefix **AD** means "toward."

    *ad*dress   *ad*just   *ad*mit

The prefix **AL** means "all."

    *al*together   *al*ways   *al*mighty

The prefix **ANTE** means "before." Take care not to confuse this with **ANTI**. If you remember the meaning of both these prefixes you should be able to work out the correct spelling of a word that starts with one of them.

    *ante*date   *ante*room   *ante*cedent

The prefix **ANTI** means "against." Take care not to confuse this with **ANTE**. If you remember the meaning of both these prefixes you should be able to work out the correct spelling of a word that starts with one of them.

    *anti*war   *anti*social   *anti*depressant

The prefix **ARCH** means "chief."

    *arch*bishop   *arch*enemy   *arch*angel

The prefix **AUTO** means "self."

    *auto*graph   *auto*biography   *auto*mobile

The prefix **BENE** means "good" or "well."

    *bene*fit   *bene*volent   *bene*factor

The prefix **BI** means "two" or "twice."

    bicycle   *bimonthly*   *bifocals*

The prefix **CIRCUM** means "around."

    circumference   *circumstance*   *circumnavigate*

The prefix **CO** means "together." There is sometimes a hyphen after this prefix to make the meaning clear.

    copilot   *co-owner*   *cooperate*

The prefix **CON** means "together."

    confer   *constellation*   *converge*

When it is added before words beginning with **L**, the prefix **CON** is changed to **COL**.

    collaborate   *collateral*   *collide*

When it is added before words beginning with **B**, **M**, or **P**, the prefix **CON** is changed to **COM**.

    combat   *commit*   *compact*

When it is added before words beginning with **R**, the prefix **CON** is changed to **COR**.

    correct   *correspond*   *correlation*

The prefix **CONTRA** means "against."

    contradict   *contravene*   *contraband*

The prefix **DE** indicates removal or reversal.

*de*frost   *de*throne   *de*caffeinated

The prefix **DIS** indicates removal or reversal.

*dis*agree   *dis*honest   *dis*trust

The prefix **EN** usually means "into."

*en*rage   *en*slave   *en*danger

The prefix **EX** means "out" or "outside of."

*ex*it   *ex*port   *ex*ternal

The prefix **EX** also means "former." The prefix is followed by a hyphen when it has this meaning.

ex-wife   *ex*-partner   *ex*-president

The prefix **EXTRA** means "beyond" or "outside of."

*extra*ordinary   *extra*terrestrial   *extra*sensory

The prefix **HYPER** means "over" or "more."

*hyper*active   *hyper*critical   *hyper*tension

The prefix **IN** sometimes means "not."

*in*human   *in*sufferable   *in*credible

The prefix **IN** can also mean "in" or "into."

*in*filtrate   *in*take   *in*grown

When it is added before words beginning with **L**, the prefix **IN** is changed to **IL**.

*il*literate   *il*legal   *il*logical

When it is added before words beginning with **B**, **M**, or **P**, the prefix **IN** is changed to **IM**.

*im*balance   *im*moral   *im*possible

> Note that the word *input* is an exception to this rule.

When it is added before words beginning with **R**, the prefix **IN** is changed to **IR**.

*ir*regular   *ir*responsible   *ir*relevant

The prefix **INTER** means "between."

*inter*national   *inter*war   *inter*ruption

The prefix **INTRA** means "within."

*intra*venous   *intra*net   *intra*mural

The prefix **MACRO** means "very large."

*macro*economics   *macro*biotic   *macro*cosm

The prefix **MAL** means "bad" or "badly."

*mal*practice   *mal*formed   *mal*administration

The prefix **MAXI** means "big" or "biggest."

*maxi*mize   *maxi*mum   *maxi*dress

The prefix **MICRO** means "very small."

*micro*scope   *micro*chip   *micro*wave

The prefix **MINI** means "small."

*mini*skirt   *mini*series   *mini*bus

The prefix **MIS** means "wrong" or "false."

*mis*behave   *mis*fortune   *mis*take

The prefix **NON** means "not."

*non*sense   *non*fiction   *non*stop

The prefix **PARA** usually means "beside" or "parallel to."

*para*medic   *para*military   *para*legal

The prefix **POST** means "after."

*post*pone   *post*graduate   *post*dated

The prefix **PRE** means "before."

*pre*arranged   *pre*war   *pre*season

The prefix **PRO** means "ahead" or "forward."

*pro*rate   *pro*active   *pro*voke

The prefix **PRO** also means "in favor of." The prefix is followed by a hyphen when it has this meaning.

pro-choice   *pro*-democracy   *pro*-European

The prefix **RE** means "again."

*re*arrange *re*read *re*heat

The prefix **SEMI** means "half."

*semi*final *semi*retirement *semi*professional

The prefix **SUB** means "under."

*sub*marine *sub*soil *sub*way

The prefix **SUPER** indicates "above," "beyond," or "extreme."

*super*human *super*market *super*star

The prefix **TELE** means "distant."

*tele*graph *tele*vision *tele*scope

The prefix **TRANS** means "across."

*trans*fer *trans*plant *trans*continental

The prefix **ULTRA** indicates "beyond" or "extreme."

*ultra*sound *ultra*modern *ultra*conservative

Building blocks at the end of words

A block of letters that regularly appears at the end of words and carries a meaning is called a **suffix**. Just like a prefix at the start of a word, a suffix can be attached to a root word or word form to create a new word with a different meaning.

For example, when the letters **LESS** are added to the end of a root word, they add the meaning of "without" to the sense of the root word.

head**less**   child**less**   life**less**

It is worth studying these building blocks and noting that they occur at the end of many English words.

The suffix **ABLE** means "able to."

break**able**   read**able**   enjoy**able**

> It is difficult to distinguish this from the suffix **IBLE**, which occurs in many words and has the same meaning. A list of the common words with each suffix is given on pages 33–34.

The suffix **AL** means "related to."

season**al**   nation**al**   tradition**al**

The suffix **ANCE** indicates a state or quality.

accept**ance**   defi**ance**   resembl**ance**

The suffix **ANT** indicates an action or condition.

resist**ant**   toler**ant**   dorm**ant**

> It is difficult to distinguish this from the suffix **ENT**, which occurs in many words and has the same meaning. A list of the common words with each suffix is given on pages 35–36.

The suffix **ARY** means "related to."

caution**ary**   revolution**ary**   document**ary**

The suffix **ATE** creates verbs indicating becoming or taking on a state.

    *hyphen**ate***   *elev**ate***   *medic**ate***

The suffix **ATION** indicates becoming or entering a state.

    *hyphen**ation***   *elev**ation***   *medic**ation***

The suffix **CRACY** means "government."

    *demo**cracy***   *auto**cracy***   *bureau**cracy***

The suffix **CRAT** means "ruler."

    *demo**crat***   *auto**crat***   *bureau**crat***

The suffix **DOM** means "state of being."

    *free**dom***   *bore**dom***   *martyr**dom***

The suffix **EE** indicates a person who is affected by or receives something.

    *interview**ee***   *evacu**ee***   *honor**ee***

The suffix **EN** means "become."

    *damp**en***   *dead**en***   *black**en***

The suffix **ENCE** indicates a state or quality.

    *resid**ence***   *abstin**ence***   *depend**ence***

The suffix **ENT** indicates an action or condition.

    *abstin**ent***   *obedi**ent***   *independ**ent***

It is difficult to distinguish this from the suffix **ANT**, which occurs in many words and has the same meaning. A list of the common words with each suffix is given on pages 35–36.

The suffix **ER** means "person from."

islander   Southerner   New Yorker

The suffix **ER** also means "person who does a job" or "thing that does a job."

driver   painter   teacher
fastener   scraper   lighter

The suffix **ESCENT** means "becoming."

adolescent   obsolescent   luminescent

The suffix **ETTE** means "small."

kitchenette   cigarette   diskette

The suffix **FUL** means "full of."

beautiful   painful   resentful

The suffix **HOOD** means "state of being."

childhood   likelihood   priesthood

The suffix **IAN** creates nouns indicating a member of a profession.

politician   magician   mathematician

The suffix **IBLE** means "able to."

*ed**ible***   *ter**rible***   *pos**sible***

> It is difficult to distinguish this from the suffix **ABLE**, which occurs in many words and has the same meaning. A list of the common words with each suffix is given on pages 33–34.

The suffix **IC** means "related to."

*atom**ic***   *perio**dic***   *rhythm**ic***

The suffix **IFICATION** creates nouns indicating an action.

*not**ification***   *clas**sification***   *clar**ification***

The suffix **IFY** creates verbs indicating an action.

*not**ify***   *clas**sify***   *clar**ify***

The suffix **ISH** means "fairly" or "rather."

*small**ish***   *young**ish***   *brown**ish***

The suffix **ISH** also means "resembling."

*tiger**ish***   *boy**ish***   *amateur**ish***

The suffix **ISM** means "action" or "condition."

*critic**ism***   *hero**ism***   *absentee**ism***

The suffix **ISM** also creates nouns indicating a prejudice.

*sex**ism***   *rac**ism***   *anti-Semit**ism***

The suffix **IST** means "doer of."

motor*ist*   solo*ist*   art*ist*

The suffix **IST** also indicates a prejudice.

sex*ist*   rac*ist*   age*ist*

The suffix **ITY** indicates a state or condition.

real*ity*   stupid*ity*   continu*ity*

The suffix **IVE** indicates a tendency toward something.

explos*ive*   act*ive*   decorat*ive*

The suffix **IZE** creates verbs indicating a change or becoming.

radical*ize*   legal*ize*   econom*ize*

The suffix **LET** means "little."

book*let*   ring*let*   pig*let*

The suffix **LIKE** means "resembling."

dog*like*   child*like*   dream*like*

The suffix **LING** means "small."

duck*ling*   gos*ling*   found*ling*

The suffix **LY** means "in this manner."

kind*ly*   friend*ly*   proper*ly*

The suffix **MENT** means "state of."

contentment   enjoyment   employment

The suffix **METER** means "measure."

thermometer   barometer   speedometer

The suffix **NESS** means "state of" or "quality of."

kindness   blindness   selfishness

The suffix **OLOGY** means "study of" or "science of."

biology   sociology   musicology

The suffix **SHIP** means "state of" or "condition of."

fellowship   dictatorship   horsemanship

The suffix **SION** means "action" or "state of."

confusion   decision   explosion

> It is difficult to distinguish this from the suffix **TION**,
> which occurs in many words and has the same meaning.
> A list of the common words with each suffix is given on
> pages 36–38.

The suffix **SOME** means "tending to."

quarrelsome   troublesome   loathsome

The suffix **TION** means "action" or "state of."

creation   production   calculation

> It is difficult to distinguish this from the suffix **SION**, which occurs in many words and has the same meaning. A list of the common words with each suffix is given on pages 36–38.

The suffix **Y** means "like" or "full of."

watery   *hilly*   *snowy*

ABLE and IBLE

The suffixes **ABLE** and **IBLE** are both quite common (although **ABLE** is more common) and have the same meaning. You should be aware of the possibility of confusing these endings and check if you are not sure which one is correct.

The table below shows some common words with each ending.

Words that end in ABLE	Words that end in IBLE
adaptable	accessible
admirable	audible
adorable	compatible
advisable	convertible
agreeable	credible
allowable	divisible
arguable	eligible
available	flexible
capable	gullible
desirable	horrible
durable	illegible
enjoyable	inaudible

Words that end in ABLE	Words that end in IBLE
enviable	indelible
excitable	inedible
flammable	invisible
hospitable	irresistible
irritable	legible
lovable	negligible
movable	plausible
notable	possible
palatable	risible
probable	sensible
suitable	tangible
tolerable	terrible
wearable	visible

A useful – but not one-hundred percent reliable – rule of thumb is that when one of these endings is added to an existing word, the spelling is **ABLE**.

adapt**able**   enjoy**able**   lov**able**

Adjectives ending in **ABLE** will form related nouns ending in **ABILITY**.

cap**able**   prob**able**   suit**able**
cap**ability**   prob**ability**   suit**ability**

However, adjectives ending **IBLE** will form related nouns ending in **IBILITY**.

gull**ible**   flex**ible**   poss**ible**
gull**ibility**   flex**ibility**   poss**ibility**

ANT and ENT

The suffixes **ANT** and **ENT** are both quite common and have the same meaning. You should be aware of the possibility of confusing these endings and check if you are not sure which one is correct.

The table below shows some common words with each ending.

Words that end in ANT	*Words that end in ENT*
abundant	absent
adamant	accident
arrogant	adjacent
assistant	affluent
blatant	ailment
brilliant	ancient
buoyant	apparent
defiant	argument
deodorant	coherent
dominant	convenient
dormant	deficient
elegant	dependent
emigrant	descent
exuberant	efficient
fragrant	eminent
hesitant	equipment
ignorant	evident
immigrant	fluent
important	implement
incessant	lenient
indignant	negligent
irritant	nutrient
migrant	opulent
militant	parent
mutant	patient

Words that end in ANT	Words that end in ENT
occupant	permanent
pleasant	precedent
poignant	president
radiant	prominent
redundant	pungent
relevant	rodent
reluctant	salient
resistant	silent
stagnant	solvent
tenant	strident
tolerant	succulent
vacant	sufficient
valiant	turbulent
vigilant	vehement

Words ending in **ANT** will form related nouns ending in **ANCE** or **ANCY**.

defi**ant**	toler**ant**	vac**ant**
defi**ance**	toler**ance**	vac**ancy**

However, words ending in **ENT** will form related nouns ending in **ENCE** or **ENCY**.

flu**ent**	opul**ent**	suffici**ent**
flu**ency**	opul**ence**	suffici**ency**

SION and TION

The suffixes **SION** and **TION** are both quite common and have the same meaning (although **TION** is more common). You should be aware of the possibility of confusing these endings and check if you are not sure which one is correct.

The table below shows some common words with each ending.

Words that end in SION	Words that end in TION
adhesion	accusation
admission	ambition
cohesion	assumption
collision	attention
collusion	audition
conclusion	caution
confusion	collection
conversion	condition
derision	congestion
dimension	decoration
discussion	direction
division	duration
erosion	emotion
evasion	equation
exclusion	evolution
excursion	exception
expansion	fiction
explosion	intention
illusion	invention
inclusion	isolation
invasion	location
mission	mention
occasion	motion
omission	nation
permission	nutrition
persuasion	option
possession	pollution
revision	relation
session	separation
tension	solution
torsion	tuition
version	vacation

Words ending in **SION** are often related to adjectives ending in **SIVE**.

expansion   *persuasion*   *permission*
expansive   *persuasive*   *permissive*

However, words ending in **TION** are often related to adjectives ending in **TIVE**.

nation   *relation*   *attention*
native   *relative*   *attentive*

Building blocks at the end of verbs

There is a small group of suffixes called **inflections** that are regularly added to the basic forms of verbs. These endings indicate either the time of action or the person performing the action.

The ending **S** is added to verbs to create what is called the **third person singular** form of the present tense – that is, the form used after "he," "she," "it" or a named person or thing when talking about present action.

cheats   *cooks*   *walks*

The ending **ING** is added to verbs to create the **present participle**, which is used to refer to present action. This form of the verb, when used as a noun, is called a **gerund**.

cheating   *mixing*   *walking*

The ending **ED** is added to most verbs to create the **past tense** and **past participle** – forms that are used when talking about action in the past.

cheated   *mixed*   *walked*

Note that some common verbs have past tenses and past participles that do not end in **ED** but that are formed in an irregular way.

bent	*spent*	*did*
gone	*done*	*fallen*

Building blocks at the end of adjectives

There are two inflection suffixes that are regularly added to the basic forms of adjectives to indicate the degree of the quality indicated by the word.

The ending **ER** is added at the end of an adjective to mean "more." This is called the **comparative** form.

*smart**er***	*green**er***	*calm**er***

The ending **EST** is added at the end of an adjective to mean "most." This is called the **superlative** form.

*smart**est***	*green**est***	*calm**est***

Note that these suffixes are generally only added to words of one or two syllables. For adjectives with more than two syllables (and some adjectives with two syllables) comparative and superlative forms are created by using the words "more" and "most."

more *beautiful*	**more** *interesting*	**more** *loyal*
most *beautiful*	**most** *interesting*	**most** *loyal*

The comparative and superlative forms of the common adjectives *good* and *bad* are formed in an irregular way.

Good	*better*	*best*
Bad	*worse*	*worst*

Building blocks at the end of nouns

The inflection suffix **S** is regularly added to the basic forms of nouns to indicate the **plural** form of the word, which indicates more than one of the thing.

cats   *dogs*   *books*

> The plural form of some words is formed slightly differently, and the rules explaining how plurals are formed are given on pages 68–70.

Spelling words that contain suffixes

Adding a suffix that begins with a consonant, such as **LESS** or **SHIP**, to a root word is usually straightforward. Neither the root word nor the suffix is changed.

help + less = helpless

However, when adding a suffix that begins with a vowel, such as **ED** or **ABLE**, to a root word you need to take more care with the spelling. Depending on the ending of the root word, you may need to add an **E**, drop an **E**, double a consonant, or change a **Y** to an **I**.

cope + ed = coped
fit + ing = fitting
deny + able = deniable

> The rules for adding vowel suffixes are given in full on pages 63–64.

Double suffixes

Sometimes a suffix can have another suffix attached to it to make an even longer word.

> abuse + ive + ness = abusiveness
> soothe + ing + ness = soothingness
> avail + able + ity = availability
> care + less + ly = carelessly
> commend + able + ly = commendably
> emotion + al + ism = emotionalism
> admit + ed + ly =admittedly
> fear + less + ness = fearlessness

Greek and Latin roots

English has many words that contain Greek and Latin roots. Some of these roots appear in many different English words, and are still used regularly to create new words.

If you can get to know these roots, how to spell them, and what they mean, you will find it a great help in your reading and writing, as well as in your spelling.

AER comes from Greek *aēr*, meaning "air." It is used in a lot of words connected with air and with flying.

    aerate   **aero**bics   **aero**dynamics

AMBI comes from the Latin word *ambo*, meaning "both."

    ambidextrous   **ambi**valent

ANTHROP comes from the Greek word *anthrōpos*, meaning "human being."

anthropology   philanthropist   lycanthropy

AQUA is the Latin word for "water."

aqualung   aquamarine   aquatic

Sometimes the second **A** in **AQUA** changes to another vowel.

aqueduct   aqueous   aquifer

ASTRO comes from the Greek word *astron*, meaning "star."

astronomy   astrology   astronaut

AUDI comes from the Latin word *audīre*, meaning "to hear."

audience   audition   auditorium

BIO comes from the Greek word *bios*, meaning "life."

biology   biography   biotechnology

CAPT and **CEPT** both come from the Latin word *capere*, meaning "to take."

capture   captivate   caption
concept   intercept   reception

CEDE comes from the Latin word *cēdere*, meaning "to go."

intercede   precede   recede

Note that some words that sound like these do not have the same ending: proceed, succeed, supersede.

CENT comes from the Latin word *centum*, meaning "hundred." A *cent* is a monetary unit in many countries, taking its name from the fact that it is worth one hundredth of the main unit of currency.

    *cent*ury   *cent*imeter   *cent*ipede

CLUDE comes from the Latin word *claudere*, meaning "to close."

    con*clude*   ex*clude*   se*cluded*

CRED comes from the Latin word *crēdere*, meaning "to believe."

    in*cred*ible   *cred*it   *cred*ulous

CYCL comes from the Latin word *cyclus*, which is derived from the Greek word *kuklos*, meaning "circle" or "wheel."

    re*cycl*able   *cycl*one   bi*cycl*e

DEC comes from the Latin word *decem*, meaning "ten."

    *dec*imal   *dec*ibel   *dec*iliter

DICT comes from the Latin word *dīcere*, meaning "to say."

    *dict*ionary   pre*dict*   contra*dict*

DOM comes from the Latin word *domus*, meaning "house."

    *dom*estic   *dom*icile   *dom*e

DOMIN comes from the Latin word *dominus*, meaning "master."

    *domin*ate   *domin*eering   con*domin*ium

DUCE and **DUCT** both come from the Latin word *ducere*, meaning "to lead."

intro**duce**   de**duce**   re**duce**
aque**duct**   con**duct**or   via**duct**

DUO is the Latin word for "two."

duo   **duo**poly   **duo**logue

EGO is the Latin word for "I."

ego   **ego**tist   **ego**centric

FACT comes from the Latin word *facere*, meaning "to make."

satis**fact**ion   **fact**ory   manu**fact**ure

FRACT comes from the Latin word *fractus*, meaning "broken."

fraction   **fract**ure   in**fract**ion

GEN comes from the Greek word *genesis*, meaning "birth."

gene   **gen**etics   **gen**esis

GEO comes from the Greek word *gē*, meaning "earth."

geology   **geo**metry   **geo**graphy

GRAPH comes from the Greek word *graphein*, meaning "to write."

graphic   auto**graph**   para**graph**

GRESS comes from the Latin word *gradī*, meaning "to go."

pro**gress**   di**gress**ion   ag**gress**ive

HYDRO comes from the Greek word *hudōr*, meaning "water."

> **hydro**plane   **hydro**foil   **hydro**therapy

Sometimes the **O** in **HYDRO** is dropped or changes to another vowel.

> **hydr**ant   **hydr**aulic   de**hydr**ated

JECT comes from the Latin word *jacere*, meaning "to throw."

> in**ject**ion   de**ject**ed   re**ject**

KILO comes from the Greek word *chīlioi*, meaning "a thousand."

> **kilo**meter   **kilo**gram   **kilo**watt

MANU comes from the Latin word *manus*, meaning "hand."

> **manu**al   **manu**facture   **manu**script

MILLI comes from the Latin word *mille*, meaning "a thousand."

> **milli**meter   **milli**gram   **milli**pede

MULTI comes from the Latin word *multus*, meaning "many."

> **multi**plication   **multi**cultural   **multi**plex

NOV comes from the Latin word *novus*, meaning "new."

> **nov**elty   re**nov**ate   in**nov**ation

OCT comes from the Latin word *octō*, meaning "eight." The Greek word is *oktō*.

> **oct**agon   **oct**ave   **oct**et

PED comes from the Greek word *pais*, meaning "child."

    encyclo**ped**ia   **ped**iatrician   **ped**ophile

PED may also come from the Latin word *pēs*, meaning "foot."

    pedal   **ped**estal   quadru**ped**

PHIL comes from the Greek word *philos*, meaning "loving."

    philanthropist   **phil**osophy   Anglo**phil**e

PHOBIA comes from the Greek word *phobos*, meaning "fear." It appears in hundreds of words relating to the fear or hatred of certain people, animals, objects, situations, and activities.

    claustro**phobia**   agora**phobia**   xeno**phobia**

PHON comes from the Greek word *phōnē*, meaning "sound" or "voice."

    phonetic   sym**phon**y   micro**phon**e

PHOTO comes from the Greek word *phōs*, meaning "light."

    photocopier   **photo**graph   **photo**sensitive

POLY comes from the Greek word *polus*, meaning "many" or "much."

    polygon   **poly**ester   **poly**gamy

PORT comes from the Latin word *portāre*, meaning "to carry."

    portable   im**port**   trans**port**ation

POS comes from the Latin word *positus*, meaning "put."

    position   im**pos**e   de**pos**it

PRIM comes from the Latin word *prīmus*, meaning "first."

    primary   **prim**itive   **prim**e

QUAD comes from the Latin word *quattuor*, meaning "four."

    quadrangle   **quad**ruped   **quad**riceps

SCOPE comes from the Greek word *skopein*, meaning "to look at."

    micro**scope**   tele**scope**   stetho**scope**

SCRIBE comes from the Latin word *scrībere*, meaning "to write."
SCRIPT comes from the Latin word *scriptus*, meaning "written," which is related to the word *scrībere*.

    scribe   sub**scribe**   de**scribe**
    script   sub**script**ion   de**script**ion

SECT comes from the Latin word *secāre*, meaning "to cut."

    section   dis**sect**   inter**sect**ion

SENT comes from the Latin word *sentīre*, meaning "to feel."

    sentimental   con**sent**   dis**sent**

SOC comes from the Latin word *socius*, meaning "friend."

    social   as**soc**iation   **soc**iology

SON comes from the Latin word *sonāre*, meaning "to sound."

    sonic   con**son**ant   re**son**ate

STAT comes from the Latin word *stātus*, meaning "standing," which itself comes from the verb *stāre*, meaning "to stand."

    *stat*ue   **stat**ic   **stat**us

STRICT comes from the Latin word *stringere*, meaning "to tighten."

    strictness   con**strict**   re**strict**ion

STRUCT comes from the Latin word *struere*, meaning "to build."

    structure   de**struct**ive   con**struct**ion

TACT comes from the Latin word *tangere*, meaning "to touch."

    tactile   con**tact**   in**tact**

TERR comes from the Latin word *terra*, meaning "earth."

    terrain   Medi**terr**anean   **terr**estrial

THERM comes from the Greek word *thermē*, meaning "heat."

    thermometer   **therm**al   hypo**therm**ia

TRACT comes from the Latin word *tractus*, meaning "dragged" or "pulled."

    con**tract**   sub**tract**ion   **tract**or

TRI comes from the Latin word *trēs*, meaning "three." The Greek word is *treis*.

    triangle   **tri**o   **tri**athlon

VEN comes from the Latin word *venīre*, meaning "to come."

*ven*ue *con*ven*tion* *inter*ven*e*

VERT comes from the Latin word *vertere*, meaning "to turn."

*di*vert *re*vert *con*vert

VIS comes from the Latin word *vīsus*, meaning "sight," which itself comes from the verb *vidēre*, meaning "to see."

vis*ual*	vis*ible*	vis*ion*
vis*it*	*super*vis*e*	*tele*vis*ion*

VOR comes from the Latin word *vorāre*, meaning "to devour."

vor*acious* *carni*vor*e* *omni*vor*ous*

Compound words

Many English words are formed simply by adding two existing words together. These are called **compound words**. It can be easy to spell these words if you break them down into their parts.

book + store = bookstore
door + mat = doormat
summer + time = summertime
tea + pot = teapot
waste + water = wastewater

Some words don't immediately seem as though they are made from two common words but in fact they are. These can also be easy to spell if you think of them in terms of their two parts.

> cup + board = cupboard
> hand + kerchief = handkerchief
> neck + lace = necklace
> pit + fall = pitfall

Commonly occurring spelling patterns

Prefixes, suffixes and root forms all can be remembered as having a particular meaning. However, there are some combinations of letters that are useful to remember when learning English spelling but that don't have any particular meaning.

The patterns in this section all appear in many different words and are not pronounced in the way you might expect. It is worth remembering these patterns and the common words in which they occur.

Some of these letter blocks were usually sounded in the original language (such as **OUGH** in Anglo-Saxon words or **IGN** in Latin words) but have lost that sound in modern English as the pronunciation of the language has gradually become simplified.

The pattern **AIN** occurs at the end of several words representing a sound that is more often spelled as **EN**. This syllable is always unstressed.

bargain	captain	certain
chaplain	curtain	fountain
mountain	porcelain	villain

The pattern **AUGHT** occurs in several words representing a sound that is more often spelled as **OT**.

aught	*caught*	*daughter*
distraught	*fraught*	*haughty*
naught	*naughty*	*onslaught*
slaughter	*taught*	

It also occurs in *laughter*, representing a sound that is more often spelled as **AFT**.

The pattern **CH** occurs in many words that come from Greek representing a sound that is more often spelled as **C** or **K**.

ache	*anchor*	*bronchitis*
chameleon	*character*	*charisma*
chasm	*chemical*	*chemistry*
chimera	*chiropractor*	*chlorine*
cholera	*cholesterol*	*chord*
choreography	*chorus*	*christen*
Christmas	*chrome*	*chronic*
monarch	*ocher*	*psychiatry*
psychology	*stomach*	*synchronize*

The pattern **CI** occurs before endings such as **OUS**, **ENT**, and **AL** in several words representing a sound that is more often spelled as **SH**. The root word often ends in **C** or **CE**.

artificial	*atrocious*	*audacious*
capricious	*commercial*	*crucial*
deficient	*delicious*	*efficient*
facial	*fallacious*	*ferocious*
financial	*gracious*	*judicious*
malicious	*official*	*officious*
pernicious	*precious*	*precocious*
proficient	*racial*	*social*

spa*cious*	spe*cial*	suffi*cient*
suspi*cious*	tena*cious*	viva*cious*

The pattern **EA** occurs in many words representing a sound that is more often spelled as **E**.

br*ea*d	br*ea*th	d*ea*f
d*ea*d	dr*ea*d	end*ea*vor
h*ea*d	h*ea*ther	h*ea*ven
h*ea*vy	l*ea*d	m*ea*dow
r*ea*dy	st*ea*dy	sw*ea*t
thr*ea*d	tr*ea*cherous	tr*ea*d
tr*ea*sure	w*ea*lth	w*ea*ther

The pattern **EAU** occurs in several words representing a sound that is more often spelled as **OW**. These words all come from French.

b*eau*	bur*eau*	chat*eau*
nouv*eau*	plat*eau*	tabl*eau*

It also occurs in these words representing a sound that is more often spelled as **EW**.

b*eau*tiful	b*eau*ty

The pattern **EIGH** occurs in several words representing a sound that is more often spelled as **AY**.

*eigh*t	fr*eigh*t	inv*eigh*
n*eigh*	n*eigh*bor	sl*eigh*
w*eigh*	w*eigh*t	

Less commonly, it can represent a sound that is more often spelled as **IE**.

h*eigh*t	sl*eigh*t

The pattern **EIGN** occurs in several words representing a sound that is more often spelled as **AIN**.

*d**eign***   *f**eign***   *r**eign***

It also occurs in these words representing a sound that is more often spelled as **IN**.

*for**eign***   *sover**eign***

The pattern **GUE** occurs at the end of several words representing a sound that is more often spelled as **G**.

*catalo**gue***	*dialo**gue***	*epilo**gue***
*fati**gue***	*haran**gue***	*intri**gue***
*lea**gue***	*merin**gue***	*monolo**gue***
*pla**gue***	*ro**gue***	*synago**gue***
*ton**gue***	*va**gue***	*vo**gue***

Some of the words above ending in **LOGUE** also have acceptable spellings that eliminate the unsounded **UE** at the end.

analog	*catalog*	*dialog*
epilog	*monolog*	*travelog*

The pattern **IGH** occurs in several words representing a sound that is more often spelled as **IE**.

*bl**igh**t*	*br**igh**t*	*f**igh**t*
*fl**igh**t*	*fr**igh**t*	*h**igh**
*l**igh**t*	*f**igh**t*	*m**igh**t*
*m**igh**ty*	*n**igh**t*	*pl**igh**t*
*r**igh**t*	*s**igh**	*s**igh**t*
*sl**igh**t*	*th**igh**	*t**igh**t*

The pattern **IGN** occurs in several words representing a sound that is more often spelled as **INE**.

al**ign**	ass**ign**	ben**ign**
cond**ign**	cons**ign**	des**ign**
mal**ign**	res**ign**	s**ign**

The pattern **OUGH** occurs in several words representing different pronunciations.

alth**ough**	bor**ough**	b**ough**
b**ough**t	br**ough**t	c**ough**
d**ough**	d**ough**ty	dr**ough**t
en**ough**	f**ough**t	**ough**t
r**ough**	s**ough**t	th**ough**
thor**ough**	th**ough**t	thr**ough**
t**ough**	tr**ough**	wr**ough**t

The pattern **OUL** occurs in several words representing a sound that is more often spelled as **OO**.

c**oul**d	sh**oul**d	w**oul**d

The pattern **OR** occurs in several words representing a sound that is more often spelled as **ER**.

arm**or**	behavi**or**	clam**or**
col**or**	demean**or**	enam**or**ed
endeav**or**	fav**or**	ferv**or**
glam**or**	harb**or**	hon**or**
hum**or**	lab**or**	neighb**or**
parl**or**	ranc**or**	rig**or**
tum**or**	vap**or**	vig**or**

Note that the spelling *glamour*, mainly a British spelling, is also used in American English.

The pattern **OUS** occurs at the end of hundreds of words representing a sound that is more naturally spelled as **US**. Note that these words are always adjectives.

anxi**ous**	cauti**ous**	danger**ous**
fabul**ous**	furi**ous**	gener**ous**
hilari**ous**	joy**ous**	mountain**ous**
ner**vous**	obvi**ous**	pi**ous**
previ**ous**	seri**ous**	zeal**ous**

The pattern **QUE** occurs in several words representing a sound that is more often spelled as **C** or **K**.

anti**que**	baro**que**	criti**que**
grotes**que**	mas**que**rade	mos**que**
opa**que**	pictures**que**	pla**que**
statues**que**	techni**que**	uni**que**

The pattern **SC** occurs in many words representing a sound that is more often spelled as **S**.

abs**ce**ss	acquie**sce**	a**sc**ent
coale**sce**	cre**sc**ent	de**sc**ent
efferve**sc**ent	fa**sc**inate	ira**sc**ible
ob**sc**ene	o**sc**illate	re**sc**ind
scene	**sc**ent	**sc**ience
scimitar	**sc**intillate	**sc**issors

The pattern **SCI** occurs before a vowel in several words representing a sound that is more often spelled as **SH**.

con**sci**ence	con**sci**ous	lu**sci**ous

The pattern **TI** occurs before endings such as **OUS**, **ENT**, and **AL** in many words representing a sound that is more often spelled as **SH**.

ambitious	cautious	contentious
circumstantial	essential	facetious
infectious	nutritious	partial
patient	potential	quotient
residential	spatial	substantial

The pattern **TURE** occurs in many words representing a sound that is often spelled as **CHER**.

adventure	capture	creature
culture	denture	feature
fracture	furniture	future
gesture	lecture	mixture
moisture	nature	pasture
picture	puncture	texture
torture	venture	vulture

spelling rules

Spelling rules

English has a small number of rules that can guide you about how words and certain types of word are spelled. If you can learn these rules, you will be on your way to becoming a better and more confident speller. Don't be put off if the rule sounds complicated – look at the examples and you will see spelling patterns emerging.

Although these rules do not cover every word in the language, they can help you make a good attempt at guessing how an unfamiliar word is spelled.

Q is always followed by U

One of the simplest and most consistent rules is that the letter **Q** is always followed by **U**.

*qu*ick   *qu*ack   *qu*iet

> The only exceptions are a few unusual words that have been borrowed from other languages, especially Arabic: bur*q*a, Ira*q*i.

J and V are followed by a vowel

These letters are rarely followed by a consonant and do not usually come at the ends of words.

If you come across a sound you think might be a **J** at the end of a word or syllable, it is likely to be spelled using the letters **GE** or **DGE**.

*pa**ge***   *e**dge***   *fora**ge***

If a word ends with the sound represented by **V**, there is likely to be a silent **E** after the **V**.

receive   *give*   *love*

Double consonants don't occur at the start of a word

If a word begins with a consonant, you can be confident that it is a single letter.

> The only exceptions are a few unusual words that have been borrowed from other languages, such as *llama*.

H, J, K, Q, V, W, X, and Y are not doubled

The consonants **B**, **C**, **D**, **F**, **G**, **L**, **M**, **N**, **P**, **R**, **S**, **T**, and **Z** are commonly doubled in the middle and at the end of words, but **H**, **J**, **K**, **Q**, **V**, **W**, **X** and **Y** are not, so you can be confident about them being single.

rejoice   *awake*   *level*

> There are occasional exceptions in compound words (such as *withhold*, *glowworm*, and *bookkeeping*), words borrowed from other languages (such as *Sukkoth and sayyid*), and informal words (such as *savvy* and *civvies*).

A, I, and U don't typically come at the end of words

In general, English avoids ending words with **A**, **I**, and **U** and adds an extra letter to stop this happening.

say   *tie*   *due*

However, there are quite a lot of exceptions to this rule, most of which are words that have been borrowed from other languages.

banana   *ravioli*   *bayou*

The three-letter rule

"Content words" (words that name and describe things and actions) have at least three letters. The only common exceptions are *go*, *do*, and *ax*. There are, however, certain informal two-letter words that are shortenings of longer words, such as *ad* (for *advertisement*), and *el* (for *elevated train*).

Note that words that do not name or describe things but exist to provide grammatical structure (prepositions, conjunctions, and determiners) can consist of one or two letters.

The three-letter rule accounts for the fact that some content words have extra or doubled letters.

buy   *bee*   *inn*

Note that these extra letters are not found in non-content words with similar sounds.

by   *be*   *in*

I before E, except after C

When the letters **I** and **E** are combined to make the "**EE**" sound, the **I** comes before the **E**.

brief	*chief*	*field*
niece	*siege*	*thief*

When these same two letters follow the letter **C** in a word, the **E** comes before the **I**.

ceiling	*deceit*	*receive*

There are a few exceptions to this rule.

caffeine	*protein*	*seize*	*weird*

The rule does not hold true when the letters **I** and **E** combine to make a sound other than "**EE**."

foreign	*surfeit*	*their*

Adding a silent E usually makes a short vowel become long

As noted on page 5, the vowels **A**, **E**, **I**, **O**, and **U** each have a "short" sound when they appear on their own in short words.

cat	*rat*	*hat*
men	*pen*	*ten*
bit	*hit*	*sit*
dot	*lot*	*got*
but	*nut*	*hut*

Each of the vowels also has a characteristic "long" sound, which is created by adding an **E** to the consonant after the vowel. The **E** is not sounded in these words.

date	*rate*	*hate*
scene	*cede*	*theme*
bite	*mite*	*like*
note	*lone*	*mole*
flute	*rule*	*brute*

If there is more than one consonant after a short vowel, adding a silent **E** does not make the vowel become long.

lapse	*cassette*	*gaffe*

C and G are soft before I and E but hard before A, O, and U

The letters **C** and **G** both have two sounds: one "soft" and one "hard."

These letters always have a hard sound when they come before **A**, **O**, and **U**.

card	*cot*	*recur*
gang	*gone*	*gum*

> Note that the word *margarine* is an exception to this rule.

In general these letters have a "soft" sound before **I** and **E** (and also **Y**).

cent	*circle*	*cycle*
gentle	*giraffe*	*gyrate*

The rule is very strong for **C**, but there are a lot of exceptions for **G**.

*gi*bbon   *gi*rl   *ge*t

Note that some words add a silent **U** after the **G** to keep the sound hard.

*gu*ess   *gu*ide   *gu*illotine
*gu*ilty   *gu*itar   fati*gue*

Adding endings to words ending in E

Many English words end with a silent **E**. When you add a suffix that begins with a vowel onto one of these words, you drop the **E**.

abbreviate + *ion* = *abbreviation*
appreciate + *ive* = *appreciative*
desire + *able* = *desirable*
fortune + *ate* = *fortunate*
guide + *ance* = *guidance*
hope + *ing* = *hoping*
response + *ible* = *responsible*
ventilate + *ed* = *ventilated*

Words that end in **CE** and **GE** are an exception to this rule. They keep the final **E** before adding a suffix that begins with **A**, **O**, or **U** in order to preserve the "soft" sound.

change + *able* = *changeable*
notice + *able* = *noticeable*
advantage + *ous* = *advantageous*

However, you do drop the **E** in these words before adding a suffix that begins with **E**, **I**, or **Y**.

> *stage + ed = staged*
> *notice + ing = noticing*
> *chance + y = chancy*

Adding the ending LY to words ending in LE

When you make an adverb by adding the suffix **LY** to an adjective that ends with **LE**, you drop the **LE** from the adjective.

> *gentle + ly = gently*
> *idle + ly = idly*
> *subtle + ly = subtly*

Adding endings to words ending in Y

When you add a suffix to a word that ends with a consonant followed by **Y**, you change the **Y** to **I**.

> *apply + ance = appliance*
> *beauty + ful = beautiful*
> *crazy + ly = crazily*
> *happy + ness = happiness*
> *smelly + er = smellier*
> *woolly + est = woolliest*

However, in certain short adjectives that end with a consonant followed by **Y**, you keep the **Y** when you add the ending **LY** to make an adverb.

> *coy + ly = coyly*
> *shy + ly = shyly*

spry + *ly* = *spry*ly
wry + *ly* = *wry*ly

Adding endings to words ending in C

You add a **K** to words that end in **C** before adding a suffix that begins with **I**, **E**, or **Y** in order to preserve the "hard" sound.

mimic + *ing* = *mimick*ing
frolic + *ed* = *frolick*ed
panic + *y* = *panick*y

The word *arc* is an exception to this rule.

arc + *ing* = *arcing*
arc + *ed* = *arced*

When you make an adverb by adding the suffix **LY** to an adjective that ends with **IC**, you add **AL** after the **IC**.

basic + *ly* = *basic**al**ly*
genetic + *ly* = *genetic**al**ly*
chronic + *ly* = *chronic**al**ly*

The word *public* is an exception to this rule.

public + *ly* = *public*ly

Adding endings to words ending in a single consonant

In **words of one syllable** ending in a short vowel plus a consonant, you double the final consonant when you add a suffix that begins with a vowel.

> *run + ing = running*
> *pot + ed = potted*
> *thin + est = thinnest*
> *swim + er = swimmer*

This rule does not apply to words ending in the consonants **H**, **J**, **K**, **Q**, **V**, **W**, **X** and **Y**, which are never doubled (see page 59).

> *slow + est = slowest*
> *box + er = boxer*

In **words of more than one syllable** ending in a single vowel plus a consonant, there are two rules.

(1) If the word is pronounced with the stress at the end, you usually double the final consonant when you add a suffix that begins with a vowel.

> *acquit + al = acquittal*
> *begin + ing = beginning*
> *commit + ed = committed*
> *occur + ence = occurrence*

(2) If the word does not have the stress at the end, you don't double the final consonant when you add a suffix that begins with a vowel.

> *target + ed = targeted*
> *darken + ing = darkening*
> *marvel + ous = marvelous*

The letter **L** generally follows the two rules given above.

> *cancel + ation = cancelation*
> *gambol + ing = gamboling*
> *marshal + ed = marshaled*
> *travel + er = traveler*
> *excel + ence = excellence*
> *repel + ent = repellent*
> *surveil + ant = surveillant*

In British English, however, **L** doubles before a suffix beginning with a vowel whether or not its syllable is stressed; thus British English spells all of the words above with double **L**. Double-**L** spellings such as *traveller* and *cancellation* are sometimes seen in American English and they are not considered incorrect.

Note that when you add a suffix that begins with a vowel to a word that ends in a single vowel plus **P**, you typically double the **P** regardless of the stress.

> *airdrop + ed = airdropped*
> *bootstrap + ed = bootstrapped*
> *handicap + ed = handicapped*
> *kidnap + er = kidnapper*
> *slip + age = slippage*
> *wrap + ing = wrapping*

Making plurals

The most common way to make a plural form of a word (to show that you are talking about more than one example of it) is simply to add an **S**.

> *dog + s = dogs*
> *house + s = houses*
> *bee + s = bees*
> *banana + s = bananas*

When you make a plural of a word that ends with **S**, **X**, **Z**, **SH**, or **CH**, you add **ES**.

> *bus + es = buses*
> *kiss + es = kisses*
> *lens + es = lenses*
> *fox + es = foxes*
> *jinx + es = jinxes*
> *buzz + es = buzzes*
> *rash + es = rashes*
> *match + es = matches*
> *ranch + es = ranches*

When you make a plural of a word that ends with a consonant plus **Y**, you change the **Y** to **I** and add **ES**.

> *fairy + es = fairies*
> *pantry + es = pantries*
> *quality + es = qualities*
> *spy + es = spies*
> *story + es = stories*

However, when you make a plural of a word that ends with a **vowel** plus **Y**, you simply add **S**.

>   boy + s = boys
>   day + s = days
>   donkey + s = donkeys
>   guy + s = guys

When you make a plural of a word that ends with a single **O**, you usually just add an **S**. This is true of nearly all words that come from Spanish.

>   bronco + s = broncos
>   memo + s = memos
>   solo + s = solos
>   taco + s = tacos
>   zero + s = zeros

However, there are a number of words that end with a single **O** that add **ES** when they are plural.

>   echo + es = echoes
>   hero + es = heroes
>   potato + es = potatoes
>   tomato + es = tomatoes
>   veto + es = vetoes

> Remember: My her**oes** eat potat**oes** and tomat**oes**.

When you make a plural of a word that ends in a single **F** (and some words that end in **FE**), you change the **F** (or **FE**) to **V** and add **ES**.

leaf + es = lea**ves**
elf + es = el**ves**
life + es = li**ves**
scarf + es = scar**ves**
self + es = sel**ves**
shelf + es = shel**ves**

There are some exceptions to this rule.

belief + s = beliefs
brief + s = briefs
chef + s = chefs
roof + s = roofs

The suffix FUL

The suffix that means "full of" is spelled **FUL** – not (as you might expect) **FULL**. When you add the suffix onto an existing word to create a new word, the new word is always spelled with just one **L**.

beautiful	cupful	faithful
grateful	hopeful	painful

The prefix AL

When *all* and another word are joined to make an unhyphenated word, you drop the second **L**.

> *all + mighty = almighty*
> *all + ready = already*
> *all + though = although*
> *all + together = altogether*

However, if the word you make by adding *all* to another word is spelled with a hyphen, you keep both **L**'s.

> *all + important = all-important*
> *all + inclusive = all-inclusive*
> *all + powerful = all-powerful*

The prefixes ANTE and ANTI

There are some English words that begin with **ANTE** and other words that begin with **ANTI**. You can usually work out how to spell the word if you think about what it means.

Words that begin with **ANTE** usually have a meaning of "before" or "in front of."

> **ante**cedent   **ante**diluvian   **ante**room

Words that begin with **ANTI** usually have a meaning of "against" or "opposite."

> **anti**septic   **anti**social   **anti**matter

The prefixes FOR and FORE

Some English words begin with **FOR** and others begin with **FORE**. You can often work out how to spell the word if you think about what it means.

Words that begin with **FORE** usually have a meaning of "before" or "in front of."

forecast   **fore**father   **fore**word

If the word does not have this meaning, it is likely that it will be spelled **FOR**, and there will not be an **E** after the **R**.

forgive   **for**get   **for**feit

The endings CE and SE

Many English words end in **CE** or **SE**. It can be easy to use the wrong spelling because **CE** and **SE** usually have the same "s" sound at the end of a word.

Here are some common words that end with a **CE** spelling.

choice	juice	niece
piece	practice	sauce
truce	vice	voice

Note that words (often adjectives) ending in **ANT** or **ENT** may have a related noun ending in **ANCE** or **ENCE**, but never in **ANSE** or **ENSE**.

defi**ant**	ignor**ant**	pati**ent**
defi**ance**	ignor**ance**	pati**ence**

Here are some common words that have **SE** at the end.

condense	*defense*	*expanse*
immense	*intense*	*license*
offense	*pretense*	*suspense*

The endings IZE and ISE

IZE is the most common suffix forming action verbs in English.

organize	*realize*	*pulverize*
stigmatize	*civilize*	*mobilize*

A few verbs sound as if they are spelled with **IZE** but in fact are spelled with **YZE**.

analyze	*catalyze*	*paralyze*

Other words are spelled with **ISE** rather than **IZE**. These are usually words where the ending is a natural part of the word and has not been added on as a suffix.

advertise	*advise*	*chastise*
comprise	*compromise*	*despise*
devise	*disguise*	*exercise*
franchise	*improvise*	*revise*
supervise	*surprise*	*televise*

Rules for using apostrophes

Showing possession

The apostrophe (') is used to show that something belongs to someone. It is usually added to the end of a word and followed by an **S**.

'S is added to the end of singular words.

> *a baby's diaper*
> *Hannah's book*
> *a child's cry*

'S is added to the end of plural words not ending in **S**.

> *children's games*
> *women's clothes*
> *people's lives*

An apostrophe alone is added to plural words ending in **S**.

> *Your grandparents are your parents' parents.*
> *We are campaigning for workers' rights.*
> *They hired a new ladies' fashion guru.*

'S is added to the end of names and singular words ending in **S**.

> *James's car*
> *the octopus's tentacles*

Note, however, that if the word ending in **S** is a historical name, an apostrophe only is sometimes preferred.

> *Dickens' novels*
> *Achilles' heel*

'S is added to the end of people or their names to indicate that you are talking about their home.

> *I'm going over to Harry's for dinner tonight.*
> *I stopped by at Mom's this afternoon, but she wasn't home.*

To test whether an apostrophe is in the right place, think about who the owner is.

> *the boy's books [= the books belonging to the boy]*
> *the boys' books [= the books belonging to the boys]*

> Note that an apostrophe is *not* used to form possessive pronouns such as *its*, *yours*, or *theirs*. Nor is it used to form the plurals of words such as *potatoes* or *tomatoes*.

Showing a contraction

An apostrophe is used in shortened forms of words to show that one or more letters have been left out. These contractions usually involve shortened forms of common verbs such as *be* and *have*.

> *I'm [short for "I am"]*
> *they've [short for "they have"]*
> *we're [short for "we are"]*

Some contractions involve the negative word *not*.

> *aren't [short for "are not"]*
> *isn't [short for "is not"]*
> *haven't [short for "have not"]*

Some contractions have two expanded forms. The context tells you which words are contracted.

he'd [short for "he had"]	*He'd already left when I got there.*
he'd [short for "he would"]	*I asked him if he'd stay.*
she's [short for "she is"]	*She's a great dancer.*
she's [short for "she has"]	*She's already eaten lunch.*

> Note that the apostrophe is always positioned at the point where the omitted letters would have been.

An apostrophe is also used in front of two digits as a way of referring to a year or decade.

China hosted the Summer Olympics in '08 [short for "2008"].
He worked as a schoolteacher during the '80s and early '90s.

Showing a plural

An apostrophe should *not* be used to form the plural of a normal word.

However, an apostrophe can be used in plurals of letters, numbers, and sometimes, in words and abbreviations spelled in all capital letters, to make them easier to read.

Mind your p's and q's.
His 2's look a bit like 7's.
She got straight A's in her exams.
There are five ATM's located on campus.

Rules for using a capital letter

A capital (or "upper-case") letter is used to mark the beginning of a sentence.

> *When I was 20, I dropped out of college and became a model.*

Capital letters are also used for the first letter in proper nouns. These include:

- people's names
  Takesha Forbes   *William Doudi*

- days of the week
  Monday   *Wednesday*   *Saturday*

- months of the year
  August   *October*   *June*

- public holidays
  Christmas   *New Year*   *Yom Kippur*

- nationalities
  Spanish   *Iraqi*   *Argentine*

- languages
  Swahili   *Flemish*   *Gaelic*

- geographical locations
  Australia   *Lake Placid*   *Mount Everest*

- religions
  Islam   *Buddhism*   *Sikhism*

Capital letters are also used for the first letter in titles of books, magazines, newspapers, **TV** shows, films, etc. Where there are several words, a capital letter is usually used for each of the main "content words" as well as the first word of the title.

The Denver Post	*Vanity **Fair***	*Twelfth Night*
The Secret Garden	*60 Minutes*	*Mamma Mia!*

tips for learning hard words

Tips for learning hard words

You can improve your spelling greatly by studying the rules and familiarizing yourself with the patterns that come up regularly. Nevertheless, knowing the principles of spelling can only get you so far. There are times when you just have to learn the order of letters in a particular word.

The tips in this chapter can help you learn tricky spellings so that they stay in your mind.

Mnemonics

A **mnemonic** is a saying or rhyme that helps you remember something. The word comes from Greek *mnēmonikos*, which itself comes from *mnēmōn*, meaning "mindful." A mnemonic can be a rhyme or sentence that helps you remember anything, not just spelling. You may already know mnemonics for other things, such as *All Cows Eat Grass*, which is often used in music as a way to remember the notes corresponding to the spaces in the bass clef (because the first letter of each word corresponds to the name of a note).

There are various types of mnemonics that can help with spelling.

Initial-letter mnemonics

In some mnemonics, the word you want to remember is spelled out by the initial letters of all the words in a sentence or phrase.

***B**ig **e**lephants **a**re **u**seful **t**o **I**ndians **f**or **u**nloading **l**ogs.*

This sentence can help you to remember the word *beautiful*.

Partial initial-letter mnemonics

In some mnemonics, a phrase acts as a reminder of how to spell only the tricky parts of a word, but does not spell out the whole word.

You can use this sort of mnemonic to remember how to spell the word *accelerate*.

*If it can **accel**erate, **a** **c**ar can **e**asily **l**ead **e**very **r**ace.*

A similar device can be used to remember the double letters in the word *accommodation*.

*The a**cc**o**mm**odations have **two** **c**ots and **two** **m**attresses.*

Partial mnemonics

Another type of mnemonic uses words or syllables that are contained within the problem word to help you remember it.

You can use this technique to remember the beginning of the word *ascertain*.

***As certain** reports are verified, we will **ascertain** the truth.*

A similar device can be used to remember the double letters at the start of the word *address*.

> **Add** your **add**ress.

The remaining chapters of this book include many mnemonics to help you remember how to spell tricky words. Use these if you find they help you.

However, the best mnemonics are often ones that you make up yourself. If you base these phrases around words and topics that are especially meaningful to you, you are more likely to remember them. For example, you might use the names of your friends, your pets, or your family members, or you might make up sentences that relate to your hobbies. Try to make up your own mnemonics for words you find hard to remember.

Look, Say, Cover, Write, Check

Another way of learning how to spell a word is to go through five
steps: look, say, cover, write, check.

- **Look** at the word carefully.

- **Say** the word aloud to yourself, listening to how it sounds.

- **Cover** the word and try to remember what it looks like.

- **Write** the word.

- **Check** what you have written to see if you got it right.

Breaking down the word into its parts

Another good way of learning a word is to break it down into its
syllables, and sound them out, pronouncing even the silent letters.

> *dictionary = dic + ti + on + ar + y*
> *ecstasy = ec + sta + sy*
> *handkerchief = hand + ker + chief*
> *material = ma + te + ri + al*
> *separate = se + par + ate*
> *Wednesday = Wed + nes + day*

If you get into the habit of looking at words in this way you will find
them easier to learn.

Word families

Words that come from the same root word tend to preserve the same core patterns in spelling. If you know that one word is related to another word, it can help you remember how the word is spelled.

The words below are all related to *act*.

act	*action*	*activity*
react	*reaction*	*reactive*

Sometimes knowing that words are related can help you remember which vowel to use. For example, words related to *irritate* all have an **A** after the **T**.

irritate	*irritant*	*irritable*

Word families are a very powerful way of remembering how to spell a word. However, there are just a few occasions when words that sound as though they might be related are in fact not related, or when words that are related are not spelled with the same core pattern. Some of these "false friends" that you need to watch out for are listed on pages 150–152.

words
with
silent
letters

Words with silent letters

Some words are hard to spell because they contain letters that are not pronounced. Often these letters were pronounced in the original language from which the word came into English. Here is a list of words that it is worth learning, including ways of remembering some of them.

abscess
    There is a silent **C** after the first **S**.
acquaint, acquiesce, acquire, acquit
    There is a silent **C** before the **Q**.
aghast
    There is a silent **H** after the **G**.

> Remember: A**gh**ast at the **gh**osts.

aisle
    There is a silent **S** before the **L**.
answer
    There is a silent **W** after the **S**.
arraign
    There is a silent **G** after the **N**.
asthma
    There is a silent **TH** after the **S**.
autumn
    There is a silent **N** after the **M**.

> Remember the adjective *autumnal* (*autumn* + *al*) where you hear the **N**.

bankruptcy
    There is a silent **T** after the **P**.

> Remember that this word comes from *bankrupt* + the ending **CY**.

Buddhism
>   There is a silent **H** after the **DD**, just as in *Buddha*.

campaign
>   There is a silent **G** before the **N**.

castle
>   There is a silent **T** after the **S**.

chalk
>   There is a silent **L** before the **K**.

column
>   There is a silent **N** after the **M**.

comb
>   There is a silent **B** after the **M**.

condemn
>   There is a silent **N** after the **M**.

> Remember that this word is related to *condemnation*.

cupboard
>   There is a silent **P** before the **B**.

> Remember that the word *clapboard* also shows this pattern:
> a *cupboard* in a *clapboard* house.

debt
>   There is a silent **B** before the **T**.

> Remember that this word is related to *debit*.

descend
>   There is a silent **C** after the **S**.

> Remember: You d**esc**end on an **esc**alator.

diaphragm
>   There is a silent **G** before the **M**.

doubt

There is a silent **B** before the **T**.

> Remember that this word is related to *dubious*.

dumb

There is a silent **B** after the **M**.

exceed, excel, excellent, excess, excite

There is a silent **C** after the **X**.

excerpt

There is a silent **C** after the **X** and a silent **P** before the **T**.

exhaust, exhibit, exhilarate

There is a silent **H** after the **X**.

extraordinary

There is a silent **A** before the **O**.

> Remember that this word comes from *extra + ordinary*.

fasten

There is a silent **T** before the **S**.

> Remember that *fasten* means "to make *fast*."

fluorescent

There is a silent **U** before the **O** and a silent **C** after the **S**.

foreign

There is a silent **G** before the **N**.

ghastly, gherkin, ghetto, ghost, ghoul

There is a silent **H** after the **G**.

gnarl, gnash, gnat, gnaw, gnome, gnu

There is a silent **G** before the **N**.

government

There is a silent **N** before the **M**.

handkerchief, handsome

There is a silent **D** after the **N**.

hasten
> There is a silent **T** after the **S**.

> Remember that *hasten* means "to make *haste*."

heir, honest, honor, hour
> There is a silent **H** at the start.

indict, indictment
> There is a silent **C** before the **T**.

> Remember: **I** **n**ever **d**abble **i**n **c**riminal **t**hings.

island, isle
> There is a silent **S** before the **L**.

jeopardize, jeopardy
> There is a silent **O** after the **E**.

knack, knead, knee, kneel, knife, knight, knit, knob, knock, knoll, knot, know, knuckle
> There is a silent **K** before the **N**.

leopard
> There is a silent **O** after the **E**.

limb, lamb
> There is a silent **B** after the **M**.

listen
> There is a silent **T** after the **S**.

medieval
> There is a silent **I** after the **D**.

miniature
> There is a silent **A** before the **T**.

mnemonic
> There is a silent **M** before the **N**.

> Remember: **M**y **n**ephew **E**ric **m**emorizes **o**dd **n**umbers **i**n **c**lass.

moreover
There is a silent **E** before the second **O**.
mortgage
There is a silent **T** before the **G**.
muscle
There is a silent **C** after the **S**.
parliament
There is a silent **A** after the **I**.
people
There is a silent **O** after the first **E**.
playwright
There is a silent **W** before the **R**.
pneumatic, pneumonia
There is a silent **P** before the **N** at the beginning.
psalm
There is a silent **P** before the **S**.
pseudonym, psychedelic, psychiatry, psychic, psychology
There is a silent **P** before the **S**.
rapport
There is a silent **T** before the second **R**.

> Remember that this word is related to *report*.

raspberry
There is a silent **P** after the **S**.
receipt
There is a silent **P** before the **T**.
**rhapsody, rhetoric, rheumatism, rhinoceros, rhododendron,
rhombus, rhubarb, rhyme, rhythm**
There is a silent **H** after the **R** at the beginning.
salmon
There is a silent **L** after the **A**.
scissors
There is a silent **C** after the first **S**.

sheikh
> There is a silent **H** after the **K**.

shepherd
> There is a silent **H** after the **P**.

> Remember that a shep**herd herd**s sheep.

silhouette
> There is a silent **H** after the **L**.

solemn
> There is a silent **N** after the **M**.

sovereign
> There is a silent **G** before the **N**.

spaghetti
> There is a silent **H** after the **G**.

stalk
> There is a silent **L** before the **K**.

subpoena
> There is a silent **B** before the **P** and a silent **O** after the **P**.

subtle
> There is a silent **B** before the **T**.

> Remember: **Sub**marines move in **sub**tle ways.

sword
> There is a silent **W** after the **S**.

talk
> There is a silent **L** before the **K**.

two
> There is a silent **W** after the **T**.

viscount
> There is a silent **S** before the **C**.

> Remember: The v**iscount** gets a d**iscount**.

walk
  There is a silent **L** before the **K**.
Wednesday
  There is a silent **D** before the **N**.
what, when, where, whether, which, why
  There is a silent **H** after the **W**.
wrangle, wrap, wrath, wreath, wreck, wrench, wrestle, wretched, wriggle, wring, wrinkle, write, wrist, wrong
  There is a silent **W** before the **R**.

single
and
double
letters

Single and double letters

Some words present a problem in spelling because it is not obvious from their pronunciation whether they have a double or single letter. Here is a list of words that it is worth learning, including ways of remembering some of them.

abbreviate
    There are two **B**'s.

> Remember: **A**lways **be b**rief when you **abb**reviate.

accelerate
    There are two **C**'s and one **L**.

> Remember: If it can **acceler**ate, **a** **c**ar **c**an **e**asily **l**ead **e**very **r**ace.

accessory
    There are two **C**'s and two **S**'s.
accident
    There are two **C**'s.

> Remember: **A** **c**lose **c**all can lead to an **acc**ident.

accommodate
    There are two **C**'s and two **M**'s.

> Remember: If you think that this word **accommodates** as many letters as possible, it will help you to remember that there are the maximum number of **C**'s and **M**'s!

accompany
    There are two **C**'s.
accumulate
    There are two **C**'s and one **M**.

accurate
There are two **C**'s and one **R**.

across
There is one **C** and two **S**'s.

acupuncture
There is only one **C** after the **A**.

address
There are two **D**'s and two **S**'s.

> Remember: **Add** your **add**ress.

affiliate
There are two **F**'s and one **L**.

aggravate
There are two **G**'s and one **V**.

aggressive
There are two **G**'s and two **S**'s.

allergy
There are two **L**'s.

> Remember: An **allergy** saps **all** en**ergy**.

alligator
There are two **L**'s and one **G**.

already, although, altogether
There is only one **L**.

aluminum
There are no double letters.

appall
There are two **P**'s and two **L**'s.

apparatus, apparent, appearance
There are two **P**'s and one **R**.

appendix, appliance, appreciate, apprehensive, approve, approximate
> There are two **P**'s.

assassinate, assess
> There are two double **S**'s.

associate
> There are two **S**'s and one **C**.

attitude
> There is a double **T** followed by a single **T**.

> Remember: **At ti**mes you have a bad **atti**tude.

baggage
> There is a double **G** – just the same as in *luggage*.

balloon
> There are two **L**'s and two **O**'s.

> Remember: A **ball**oon is shaped like a **ball**.

banana
> There are two single **N**'s.

battalion
> There are two **T**'s and one **L** – just the same as in *battle*.

beginner
> There is one **G** and two **N**'s.

bellicose, belligerent
> There are two **L**'s.

boycott
> There are two **T**'s.

broccoli
> There are two **C**'s and one **L**.

> Remember: Bro**cc**oli **c**ures **coli**c.

bulletin
> There are two **L**'s and one **T** – just the same as in *bullet*.

carafe
> There is one **R** and one **F**.

career
> There is no double **R**.

> Remember: A **car car**eered off the road.

cassette
> There are two **S**'s and two **T**'s.

cinnamon
> There are two **N**'s and one **M**.

collaborate
> There are two **L**'s and one **B**.

colleague
> There are two **L**'s.

colonnade
> There is one **L** and two **N**'s.

colossal
> There is one **L** in the middle and two **S**'s.

> Remember: Co**loss**al **loss**es

commemorate
> There is a double **M** followed by a single **M**.

commercial
> There are two **M**'s.

commiserate
> There are two **M**'s and one **S**.

commit
> There are two **M**'s and one **T**.

committee
> There are two **M**'s, two **T**'s, and two **E**'s.

> If you remember that a **committee** should have as many members as possible, it may help you remember that this word has the maximum number of **M**'s, **T**'s, and **E**'s.

commotion
> There are two **M**'s (unlike *locomotion*).

compel
> There is only one **L** (but the **L** doubles when most inflections are added).

connotation
> There are two **N**'s and two single **T**'s.

control
> There is only one **L** (but the **L** doubles when most inflections are added).

coolly
> There are two **L**'s.

> Remember: This word is *cool* + the ending **LY**.

correspond
> There are two **R**'s.

curriculum
> There are two **R**'s and one **C** in the middle.

daffodil
> There are two **F**'s but no double **D** or **L**.

desiccated
> There is one **S** and two **C**'s – which is the same as in *coconuts*!

deterrent
> There are two **R**'s but no double **T**.

dilemma
> There is one **L** and two **M**'s.

> Remember: **Emma** is in a dil**emma**.

disappear, disappoint, disapprove
> There is one **S** and two **P**'s.

> Remember: Th**is app**le has d**isapp**eared.

dispel
> There is one **S** and only one **L**.

dissatisfied
> There are two **S**'s after the first **I**.

dissect
> There are two **S**'s.

dissimilar
> There are two **S**'s, one **M**, and one **L**.

dumbbell
> There are two **B**'s.

> Remember: This is a compound of *dumb* and *bell*.

earring
> There are two **R**'s.

> Remember: This is a compound of *ear* and *ring*.

effervescent
> There are two **F**'s and one **S**.

eligible
> There is only one **L** at the start.

> Remember: You must **el**ect the most **el**igible candidate:
> **El**i.

embarrass
There are two **R**'s and two **S**'s.

> Remember: This word has two **R**'s and two **S**'s, which is an **embarrass**ment of riches!

enroll
There are two **L**'s.

> Remember: When you en**roll** your name will be on a **roll**.

erroneous
There are two **R**'s and one **N**.

> Remember that this word is related to *err*.

exaggerate
There are two **G**'s.

> Remember: I am st**agger**ed by how much you ex**agger**ate.

excellent
There are two **L**'s.

> Remember: My **ex-cell**mate was an **excell**ent friend.

flammable
There are two **M**'s (unlike *flame*).

fullness
There are two **L**'s and two **S**'s.

giraffe
There is one **R** and two **F**'s.

guerrilla
There are two **R**'s and two **L**'s.

graffiti
There are two **F**'s and one **T**.

hallucination
There are two **L**'s, one **C**, and one **N**.

harass
There is one **R** and two **S**'s.

hazard
There is only one **Z** (unlike *blizzard*).

hideous
There is only one **D**.

> Remember: **Hide** that **hide**ous thing away.

holiday
There is only one **L** and one **D**.

> Remember that a hol**id**ay was originally a holy **d**ay.

horrible
There are two **R**'s – just the same as in *terrible*.

horror
There is a double **R** – just the same as in *terror*.

hurricane
There are two **R**'s and one **C**.

illiterate
There are two **L**'s and a single **T**.

imitate
There are no double letters.

immediate
There are two **M**'s and one **D**.

inaccurate
There is one **N**, two **C**'s, and one **R**.

ineligible
There are no double letters.

innocent
> There are two **N**'s and one **C**.

innocuous
> There are two **N**'s and one **C**.

intelligence, intelligent
> There are two **L**'s.

> Remember: I can **tell** the **gent** is in**tell**igent.

interrogate
> There are two **R**'s and one **G**.

> Remember: In**terro**gation may cause **terro**r.

interrupt
> There are two **R**'s.

> Remember: It's **terri**bly rude to in**terr**upt.

irascible
> There is only one **R**.

> Remember that this word is related to *irate*, which also has only one **R**.

irregular
> There are two **R**'s and one **G**.

irrelevant
> There are two **R**'s and one **L**.

irritable
> There are two **R**'s and one **T**.

limit
> There is only one **M** and one **T**.

literature
> There is only one **T**.

luggage

There is a double **G** – just the same as in *baggage*.

macabre

There is only one **C**.

macaroon

There is only one **C** and one **R**.

> Remember: Ma**car**oons taste great after ma**car**oni.

mattress

There are two **T**'s and two **S**'s.

mayonnaise

There are two **N**'s.

> Remember: Dip **n**ice **n**ibbles in mayo**nn**aise.

Mediterranean

There is one **D**, one **T**, and two **R**'s.

millennium

There are two **L**'s and two **N**'s.

millionaire

There are two **L**'s and one **N**.

misshapen

There are two **S**'s.

misspell

There are two **S**'s and two **L**'s.

misspent

There are two **S**'s.

moccasin

There are two **C**'s and one **S**.

necessary

There is one **C** and two **S**'s.

> Remember: It is ne**cess**ary for a shirt to have **one c**ollar
> and **two s**leeves.

obsession, obsessive
There is a single **S** followed by a double **S**.

occasion
There are two **C**'s and one **S**.

occupy
There are two **C**'s and one **P**.

occur
There are two **C**'s and one **R**.

occurrence
There are two **C**'s and two **R**'s.

omission
There is one **M** and two **S**'s.

opinion
There is one **P** and a single **N** in the middle.

opponent, opportunity, opposite
There are two **P**'s.

overrate
There are two **R**'s – just the same as in *underrate*.

paraffin
There is one **R** and two **F**'s.

parallel
There is a double **L** in the middle and a single **L** at the end.

pastime
There is one **S** and one **T**.

pavilion
There is only one **L**.

penicillin
There are two **L**'s and no double **N**.

> Remember: You take penic**ill**in when you are **ill**.

permit
There is only one **T**.

personnel
There are two **N**'s and one **L**.

porridge

There are two **R**'s.

possess

There are two double **S**'s.

> Remember: You should po**ss**ess **two s**hoes and **two s**ocks.

possible

There are two **S**'s.

preferred

There is one **F** and a double **R**.

preference

There is one **F** and no double **R**.

procedure

There is only one **E** after the **C**.

profession, professor

There is one **F** and two **S**'s.

profitable

There is one **F** and one **T**.

propel

There is a single **P** in the middle, and a single **L**.

propeller

There is a single **P** in the middle, and a double **L**.

quarrel

There are two **R**'s and one **L**.

questionnaire

There are two **N**'s.

really

There are two **L**'s.

> Remember: This word is *real* + the ending **LY**.

rebellion

There is one **B** and two **L**'s.

recommend
There is one **C** and two **M**'s.
recurrent
There is a single **C** and a double **R**.
referred
There is a single **F** and a double **R**.
remittance
There is one **M** and two **T**'s.
resurrection
There is a single **S** and a double **R**.
sapphire
There are two **P**'s.

Remember: You would be ha**pp**y to get a sa**pp**hire.

satellite
There is one **T** and two **L**'s.

Remember: **Tell** me about the sa**tell**ite.

scissors
There is a double **S** in the middle.
skillful
There is a double **L** and then a single **L**.

Remember: Just as in *skill*.

solicitor
There are no double letters.
success
There is a double **C** and a double **S**.
succinct
There is a double **C**.
suddenness
There is a double **D** and a double **N**.

sufficient
> There are two **F**'s.

suffocate
> There are two **F**'s and one **C**.

supplement
> There are two **P**'s and one **M**.

suppose
> There are two **P**'s.

suppress
> There is a double **P** and a double **S**.

surplus
> There is only one **S** at the end.

symmetry
> There are two **M**'s and one **T**.

taffeta
> There are two **F**'s and no double **T**.

tattoo
> There is a double **T** and a double **O**.

terrible
> There are two **R**'s – just the same as in *horrible*.

terror
> There is a double **R** – just the same as in *horror*.

threshold
> There is no double **H**.

toffee
> There are two **F**'s and two **E**'s.

tomorrow
> There is one **M** and two **R**'s.

tranquil
> There is only one **L** at the end.

tyranny
> There is one **R** and two **N**'s.

underrate
> There are two **R**'s – just the same as in *overrate*.

until
> There is only one **L** at the end.

usually
> There are two **L**'s.

> Remember: This word is *usual* + the ending **LY**.

vacuum
> There is one **C** and two **U**'s.

vanilla
> There is one **N** and two **L**'s.

> Remember: **Vanill**a ice cream from the **van** made me **ill**.

villain
> There are two **L**'s.

walnut
> There is only one **L** and one **T**.

welcome, welfare
> There is only one **L**.

withhold
> There are two **H**'s.

words
with
foreign
spelling
patterns

Words with foreign spelling patterns

Some words present a problem in spelling because they have come into English from another language and have kept a spelling pattern found in the original language. Often these spelling patterns are quite different from the patterns you would expect to find in English words.

If you know a bit of French or Greek, for example, you will find it easier to understand why words that come from those languages are spelled the way they are. Even if you don't, you should soon get used to certain spelling patterns from these languages that appear repeatedly in English, such as **EAU** and **EUR** in French words and **PH** and **RRH** in Greek words.

Here is a list of words that it is worth learning, including ways of remembering some of them.

aficionado
    There is one **F** and the middle is **CIO**. The word comes from Spanish.
amateur
    The ending is **EUR**. The word comes from French.
apparatus
    The ending is **US** (not **OUS**). The word comes from Latin.
archaeology
    The second syllable is spelled **CHAE**. The word comes from Greek.

> Remember: Ar**chae**ology discovers **c**urious **h**ouses of **a**ncient **e**ras.

beautiful, beauty
    The beginning is **BEAU**. These words come from French.

> Remember: **B**ig **e**ars **a**re **u**seful.

beige
    The ending is **EIGE**. The word comes from French.

biscuit

> The ending is **CUIT**. The word comes from French (where *cuit* means "cooked").

> Remember: If you want a bis**cuit**, I will give **u it**.

bouquet

> The first vowel sound is spelled **OU**, the middle consonant is **Q**, and the ending is **ET**. The word comes from French.

> Remember: A bou**que**t for a **que**en.

bourgeois

> The first vowel sound is spelled **OUR**, the consonant in the middle is **GE**, and the ending is **OIS**. The word comes from French.

Braille

> The ending is **AILLE**. The word comes from a French name.

brochure

> The ending is **CHURE**. The word comes from French.

brusque

> The ending is **SQUE**. The word comes from French.

bureau

> The ending is **EAU**. The word comes from French.

> Remember: **B**usinesses **u**sing **r**otten **e**thics **a**re **u**seless.

camaraderie

> The first three vowels are **A**. Until the last two letters, the pattern *consonant + vowel* is repeated 5 times. The word comes from French.

camouflage

> The vowel sound in the middle is spelled **OU**, and the ending is **AGE**. The word comes from French.

catarrh

> The ending is **ARRH**. The word comes from Greek.

champagne
The opening is **CH** and the ending is **AGNE**. The word comes from a French place-name.

chaos
The opening sound is spelled **CH**. The word comes from Greek.

Remember: **C**riminals **h**ave **a**bandoned **o**ur **s**ociety.

character
The opening sound is spelled **CH**. The word comes from Greek.

chauffeur
The opening is **CH** and the ending is **EUR**. The word comes from French.

chord, chorus
The opening sound is spelled **CH**. These words come from Greek.

chute
The opening is **CH**. The word comes from French.

connoisseur
The middle vowel sound is spelled **OI** and the final vowel sound is spelled **EUR**. The word comes from French. (Also watch out for the double **N** and double **S**!)

crochet
The ending is **CHET**. The word comes from French.

dachshund
The middle is **CHSH**. The word comes from German (where *Dachs* means "badger" and *Hund* means "dog").

Remember: Da**chsh**un**d**s **ch**ase **sh**eep through the **und**ergrowth.

diarrhea
The middle is **RRHE**. The word comes from Greek.

etiquette
The ending is **QUETTE**. The word comes from French.

euphoria, euthanasia

The opening is **EU**. These words come from Greek (where *eu* means "well").

Fahrenheit

There is an **H** before the **R**, and the ending is **EIT**. The word comes from a German name.

fiancé, fiancée

The ending is **CÉ** when referring to a man and **CÉE** when referring to a woman. The word comes from French.

foyer

The ending is **ER**. The word comes from French.

gateau

The ending is **EAU**. The word comes from French.

grandeur

The ending is **EUR**. The word comes from French.

hemorrhage

The middle is **ORRH**. The word comes from Greek.

hierarchy, hieroglyphics

The beginning is **HIER**. These words come from Greek (where *hieros* means "holy").

> Remember: **H**idden **i**n **E**gyptian **r**uins.

hypochondriac, hypocrisy, hypocrite

The beginning is **HYPO**. These words come from Greek (where *hypo* means "under").

jodhpur

There is a silent **H** after the **D** and the ending is **UR**. The word comes from a place name in India.

> Remember: You wear jo**dh**purs when you ride a **d**appled **h**orse.

karate

The final letter is **E**. The word comes from Japanese.

khaki
There are two **K**'s and a silent **H**. The word comes from Urdu.

larynx
The ending is **YNX**. The word comes from Greek.

lasagne
The ending is **AGNE**. The word comes from Italian. The spelling *lasagna* is also used.

lieutenant
The first vowel sound is spelled **IEU**. The word comes from French (where *lieu* means "place").

liqueur
The ending is **QUEUR**. The word comes from French.

machete
The middle sound is spelled **CH**. The final vowel is **E**. The word comes from Spanish.

maneuver
The vowel sound in the middle is spelled **EU**. The word comes from French.

martyr
The ending is **YR**. The word comes from Greek.

matinée
The ending is **ÉE** – just the same as in *fiancée*. The word comes from French.

meringue
The ending is **INGUE**. The word comes from French.

memoir
The ending is **OIR**. The word comes from French.

mustache
The ending is **CHE**. The word comes from French.

naïve
The middle of this word is **AÏ**. The word comes from French.

niche
The ending is **ICHE**. The word comes from French.

nuance
The vowel after **U** is **A**. The word comes from French.

omelette

There is an **E** after the **M** and the ending is **ETTE**. The word comes from French. The simpler spelling *omelet* is also used.

pseudonym

There is a silent **P** at the beginning, the first vowel sound is spelled **EU**, and the ending is **NYM**. The word comes from Greek.

psychiatry, psychic, psychology

There is a silent **P** at the beginning, the first vowel is a **Y**, and there is an **H** after the **C**. These words come from Greek (where *psychē* means "soul").

queue

The sequence of vowels is **UEUE**. The word comes from French, where it means "tail."

reconnaissance

The third vowel sound is spelled **AI**. The word comes from French. (Also watch out for the double **N** and double **S** – just the same as in *connoisseur*.)

rendezvous

The first vowel sound is spelled **E**, the second is spelled **EZ**, and the ending is **OUS**. The word comes from French.

repertoire

The middle vowel sound is spelled **ER** and the ending is **OIRE**. The word comes from French.

reservoir

The middle sound is spelled **ER** and the ending is **OIR**. The middle **R** is not always pronounced. The word comes from French.

> Remember: A **reserv**oir **reserv**es water.

restaurant

The middle vowel sound is spelled **AU** and the ending is **ANT**. The word comes from French.

restaurateur

There is no **N** before the second **T** (unlike in *restaurant*), and the ending is **EUR**. The word comes from French.

rheumatism
> The opening is **RHEU**. The word comes from Greek.

rhinoceros
> The opening is **RH**, and the ending is **OS**. The word comes from Greek.

schizophrenia
> The opening is **SCH**, and the next consonant sound is spelled with **Z**. The word comes from Greek (where *schizein* means "to split").

sheikh
> The vowel sound is spelled **EI**, and there is a silent **H** at the end. The word comes from Arabic.

silhouette
> There is a silent **H** after the **L**, the middle vowel is spelled **OU**, and the ending is **ETTE**. The word comes from French.

souvenir
> The first vowel sound is spelled **OU** and the ending is **IR**. The word comes from French.

spaghetti
> There is a silent **H** after the **G** and the ending is **ETTI**. The word comes from Italian (as does *confetti*, which has a similar ending).

suede
> The ending is **UEDE**. The word comes from French (where *de Suède* means "Swedish").

> Remember: **Sue de**manded **suede** shoes.

surveillance
> The middle vowel sound is spelled **EI**. The word comes from French.

ukulele
> The first two vowels are **U**; the last two are **E**. The word comes from Hawaiian.

yacht
> The middle is **ACH**. The word comes from Dutch.

confusable words

Confusable words

When two words have a similar or identical sound, it is easy to confuse them and use the correct spelling for the wrong word. This section lists sets of words that are easily confused and offers some ways of remembering which is which.

accept, except
To **accept** something is to receive it or agree to it. **Except** means "other than" or "apart from."

> Please **accept** my apologies
> The mayor would not **accept** their demands.
> I never wear a skirt **except** when we go out.

affect, effect
To **affect** something is to influence or change it. An **effect** is a result something gives or an impression something makes.

> Tiredness **affected** his concentration.
> discoveries that have a profound **effect** on medicine

> Remember: To **a**ffect something is to **a**lter it but the **e**ffect is the **e**nd result. Another mnemonic for this difference is the word **raven**. **R**emember, **a**ffect **v**erb, **e**ffect **n**oun.

aid, aide
Aid means "help," and to **aid** somebody is to help them. An **aide** is a person who acts as an assistant to an important person.

> bringing **aid** to victims of drought
> They used fake uniforms to **aid** them in the robbery.
> one of the President's **aides**

aloud, allowed

Aloud means "loud enough to hear." **Allowed** is the past tense of the verb **allow**, and is also used as an adjective.

> Read your sentence **aloud** to the class.
> Who **allowed** them onto the property?
> a list of **allowed** commands.

allude, elude

To **allude** to something is to refer to it in an indirect way. If something **eludes** you, you can't understand or remember it, and if you **elude** something, you dodge or escape from it.

> I never **allude** to that unpleasant matter.
> The name of the tune **eludes** me.
> She managed to **elude** the police.

> Remember: If something **e**ludes you, it **e**scapes you.

altar, alter

An **altar** is a holy table in a church or temple. To **alter** something is to change it.

> The church has a magnificent **altar**.
> We may have to **alter** our plans.

ascent, assent

An **ascent** is an upward climb. To **assent** to something is to agree to it, and **assent** means "agreement."

> the **ascent** of Mount Everest
> We all **assented** to the plan.
> You have my whole-hearted **assent**.

aural, oral
Something that is **aural** is to do with the ear or listening. Something that is **oral** is to do with the mouth or speaking.

> *a good **aural** memory*
> ***oral** history*

Remember: An **au**ral examination might involve **au**dio equipment.

base, bass
The **base** of something is the bottom part of it. A **bass** voice or instrument is the one that produces the lowest musical notes.

> *the **base** of the table*
> *a **bass** guitar*

baited, bated
If something such as a hook is **baited**, it has food attached to it as a temptation. The word **bated** means "cut short," and is mainly used in the expression *bated breath*.

> *The trap had been **baited**.*
> *I waited with **bated** breath.*

berth, birth
A **berth** is a bed on a ship or train, or a place where a ship is tied up. The **birth** of someone or something is the act of it being born or created.

> *a cabin with six **berths***
> *the date of her **birth***
> *the **birth** of jazz*

board, bored
A **board** is a long piece of wood, or a group of people with authority. *Bored* means impatient and uninterested. *Bored* is also the past tense of the verb *bore*.

*A **board** was nailed across the door.*
*She sits on the **board** of directors.*
*I've been feeling **bored** all afternoon.*
*Carpenter bees **bored** holes in the wood.*

born, borne

To be **born** is to be brought into life. To be **borne** is to be accepted or carried, and when fruit or flowers are **borne** by a plant, they are produced by it. If something is **borne** out, it is confirmed.

*Olivia was **born** in Houston.*
*He has **borne** his illness with courage.*
*The trees have **borne** fruit.*
*The predictions have been **borne** out by the election results.*

boulder, bolder

A **boulder** is a large rock. The word **bolder** means "more brave" or "more daring."

*The road was blocked by an enormous **boulder**.*
*The victory made the soldiers feel **bolder**.*

bow, bough

To **bow** is to bend your body or head, and a *bow* is an action where you bend your body or head. A *bough* is a branch of a tree.

*He gave a long **bow** to the king.*
*overhanging **boughs** of elm and ash*

brake, break

A **brake** is a device for slowing down, and to **brake** is to slow down by using this device. To **break** something is to change it so that it does not work or exist.

*I slammed on the **brakes**.*
***Brake** when you approach the intersection.*
*Don't **break** that vase!*

breach, breech
To **breach** something is to break or break through it, and a **breach** is a break or a gap made. The **breech** is the lower part of a human body, a rifle, or some other thing.

> *a **breach** of the peace*
> *In a **breech** birth the baby's legs come out first.*

breath, breathe
Breath, without an **E**, is the noun, but **breathe**, with an **E**, is the verb.

> *He took a deep **breath**.*
> *I heard him **breathe** a sigh of relief.*

bridal, bridle
Bridal means "relating to a bride." A **bridle** is a piece of equipment for controlling a horse, and to **bridle** at something means to show anger about it.

> *a **bridal** dress*
> *a leather **bridle***
> *I **bridled** at the suggestion that I had been dishonest.*

broach, brooch
To **broach** a difficult subject means to introduce it into a discussion. A **brooch** is an item of jewelry.

> *Every time I **broach** the subject, he walks away.*
> *a diamond **brooch***

callous, callus
Someone who is **callous** does not take other people's feelings into account. A **callus** is a patch of hard skin.

> *He treats her with **callous** rudeness.*
> *Wearing high heels can cause **calluses**.*

cannon, canon

A **cannon** is a large gun that fires heavy balls. A **canon** is a general rule or an official collection of texts.

> The ship fired its only *canvas*.
> the *canon* of great American novels

canvas, canvass

Canvas is strong cloth. To **canvass** is to persuade people to vote a particular way or to find out their opinions about something.

> a *canvas* bag
> The store decided to *canvass*, its customers.

> Remember: If you canva**ss**, you **s**eek **s**omething.

capital, capitol

A **capital** is a city that is also a seat of government. A **capitol** is a building that is a government headquarters. **Capitol** is often **capitalized** (that is, it starts with a **capital** letter).

> What's the *capital* of Delaware?
> The *Capitol* is decorated with beautiful lights at Christmas.

> Remember: The **Capitol** has a r**o**und d**o**me.

cereal, serial

Cereal is food made from grain. A **serial** is something published or broadcast in a number of parts. **Serial** also describes other things that happen in a series.

> my favorite breakfast *cereal*
> a three-part *serial*
> a *serial* offender

Remember: A **seri**al is a part of a **seri**es, but a ce**real** is a **real** breakfast.

chord, cord
A **chord** is a group of three or more musical notes played together.
Cord is strong thick string or electrical wire. Your vocal **cords** are folds in your throat that are used to produce sound.

> *major and minor **chords***
> *tied with a thick **cord***

Remember: A **chor**us often sings **chor**ds.

chute, shoot
A **chute** is a steep slope for sliding things down. To **shoot** something means to send a missile at it, and to **shoot** means to go very fast. A **shoot** is also a very young plant.

> *a laundry **chute***
> ***shooting** at pigeons*
> *to **shoot** along the ground*
> *bamboo **shoots***

coarse, course
Coarse means "rough" or "rude." A **course** is something that you go around, or a set of classes in which you learn something. **Course** is also used in the phrase *of course*.

> *a **coarse** fabric*
> *his **coarse** jokes*
> *a golf **course***
> *a meditation **course***
> *Of **course** I want to go with you.*

colander, calendar
A **colander** is a bowl-shaped drainer. A **calendar** is a chart with dates on it.

*Strain the potatoes with a **colander**.*
*a **calendar** with mountain scenes*

> Remember: A col**ander** has h**and**les and drains wat**er**, while the cal**endar** marks the **end** of the ye**ar**.

complement, compliment

A **complement** is something that goes well with something else or that completes it, and to **complement** something is to go well with it or complete it. A **compliment** is a remark expressing admiration, and to **compliment** something is to express admiration for it.

*She is a perfect **complement** to her husband.*
*The host received many **compliments** on the food.*

> Remember: A compl**i**ment is the opposite of an **i**nsult and a compl**e**ment compl**e**tes something.

confidant, confident

A **confidant** is a friend you tell secrets to. **Confident** means "trusting" or "self-assured."

*a trusted **confidant***
*We are **confident** you will do a good job.*

council, counsel

A **council** is a group of people elected to look after the affairs of an area. **Counsel** is advice and to **counsel** is to give advice.

*the city **council***
*I **counseled** her to forgive him.*

> Remember: The coun**cil** members take minutes with pen**cil**s.

councilor, counselor
A **councilor** is a member of a council. A **counselor** is someone who gives advice, especially a lawyer. Both words are sometimes spelled with **LL**.

> Three **councilors** resigned after the meeting.
> The college assigns each student a **counselor**.

currant, current
A **currant** is a small berry. A **current** is a flow of water, air, or electricity. **Current** also means happening.

> a **currant** bush
> an electrical **current**

> Remember: There are curr**a**nts in c**a**kes and curr**e**nts in **e**lectricity.

dairy, diary
A **dairy** is a place where milk is processed. **Dairy** products are foods made from milk. A **diary** is a book in which you write down thoughts and events.

> She worked in a **dairy**.
> an entry in her **diary**.

> Remember: The d**airy** next to the **air**port.

decease, disease
The verb **decease** means "to die." A **disease** is an unhealthy condition.

> my **deceased** father
> an infectious **disease**

> Remember that if you are de**ceased** you have **ceased** to be.

defuse, diffuse

To **defuse** something is to make it less dangerous or tense. To **diffuse** something is to spread it or cause it to scatter. **Diffuse** means spread over a wide area.

> Police **defused** a powerful bomb.
> The governor will try to **defuse** the crisis.
> The message was **diffused** widely.
> curtains to **diffuse** the glare of the sun

desert, dessert

A **desert** is a region that receives little rain. To **desert** someone is to abandon them. A **dessert** is sweet food served after the main course of a meal.

> the Mojave **Desert**
> She **deserted** me to go shopping.
> We had apple pie for **dessert**.

Remember: A de**ss**ert is a **s**ticky **s**weet food.

device, devise

Device, with a **C**, is the noun. **Devise**, with an **S**, is the verb.

> a safety **device**
> The schedule that you **devise** must be flexible.

discreet, discrete

If you are **discreet** you do not cause embarrassment with private matters. **Discrete** things are separate or distinct.

> We made **discreet** inquiries.
> The job was broken down into several **discrete** tasks.

Remember: When discr**e**t**e** means "separate," the **E**'s are separate.

elegy, eulogy
An **elegy** is a mournful song or poem. A **eulogy** is a speech praising someone or something, especially someone who has just died.

> *elegies of love and loss*
> *His nephew delivered a nostalgic eulogy*

elicit, illicit
To **elicit** something such as information means to draw it out.
If something is **illicit**, it is not allowed.

> *I managed to elicit the man's name.*
> *illicit drugs*

eligible, illegible
Eligible means "suitable to be chosen for something." If something is difficult to read, it is **illegible**.

> *an eligible candidate*
> *illegible handwriting*

> Remember: **El**igible means suitable to be chosen, and so is related to the word **el**ect.

emigrate, immigrate
If you **emigrate**, you leave a country to live somewhere else. Someone who does this is an **emigrant**. If you **immigrate**, you enter a country to live there. Someone who does this is an **immigrant**.

> *Her parents had emigrated from Scotland.*
> *Russian immigrants living in the United States*

> Remember: **I**mmigrants come **i**n.

eminent, imminent
Someone who is **eminent** is well-known and respected. **Imminent** means "about to happen."

> an **eminent** professor
> an **imminent** disaster

emit, omit

If something is **emitted**, it is let out. If you **omit** something, you leave it out. Similarly, something that is let out or sent out is an **emission**, while something that is left out is an **omission**.

> cars **emitting** exhaust fumes
> She was **omitted** from the team.
> a program to cut carbon **emissions**
> a surprising **omission** from the list of great painters

enquire, inquire

These are alternative spellings for the same word. You can spell this word with an **E** or an **I**, although the form **inquire** is more common. Some people use the form **enquire** to mean "ask about" and the form **inquire** to mean "investigate."

ensure, insure

To **ensure** that something happens is to make sure that it happens. To **insure** something is to take out financial cover against its loss. To **insure** against something is to do something in order to prevent it or protect yourself from it.

> His performance **ensured** victory for his team.
> You can **insure** against identify theft.
> Football teams cannot **insure** against the cancelation of a game.

envelop, envelope

Envelop is the verb meaning "to cover or surround." **Envelope**, with an **E** at the end, is the noun meaning "a paper covering that holds a letter."

> Mist began to **envelop** the hills.
> a self-addressed **envelope**

exercise, exorcize

To **exercise** means to move energetically, and **exercise** is a period of energetic movement. To **exorcize** an evil spirit means to get rid of it.

> Remember: You ex**e**rcise your l**e**gs but ex**o**rcize a gh**o**st.

faun, fawn

A **faun** is a legendary creature. A **fawn** is a baby deer. To **fawn** on or over someone is to flatter them.

> *a story about **fauns** and centaurs*
> *Bambi the **fawn***
> ***fawning** over his new boss*

faze, phase

Faze is a verb meaning "disturb" and is almost always used with "not." **Phase** is a noun that denotes a stage in a process.

> *He wasn't **fazed** by the bad news.*
> *teenagers going through a rebellious **phase***

final, finale

Final means "last of a series," and a **final** is the last game or contest in a series to decide the winner. A **finale**, with an **E** at the end, is the finish of something, especially the last part of a piece of music or a show.

> *the World Cup **Final***
> *the **finale** of a James Bond film*

flare, flair

Flair is ability. A **flare** is a bright torch used as a warning, and to **flare** is also to widen out.

> *She showed natural **flair**.*
> ***flared** jeans*

flour, flower
Flour is used in baking. A **flower** is the colored part of a plant.

> *self-rising **flour***
> *a basket of **flowers***

> Remember: Flo**u**r makes bis**c**u**i**ts and d**u**mplings.

forgo, forego
To **forgo** means to choose not to have something. To **forego** is a less common word meaning "to go before."

> *I decided to **forgo** the pudding.*
> *I will ignore the **foregoing** remarks.*

fowl, foul
Foul means dirty or unpleasant, and a **foul** is an illegal action in a sport. **Fowl** are certain types of birds that can be eaten.

> ***foul** play*
> *called for a bad **foul***
> *a butcher selling wild **fowl***

gambol, gamble
To **gambol** means to run about friskily. To **gamble** means to accept a risk, and a **gamble** is a risk that you take.

> *lambs **gamboling** on the hillside*
> *to **gamble** on horses*
> *Going there would be an enormous **gamble**.*

gorilla, guerrilla
A **gorilla** is a large ape. A **guerrilla** is a member of a small unofficial army fighting an official one.

> *a documentary about **gorillas** and chimps*
> *ambushed by a band of **guerrillas***

> Remember: King K**o**ng was a giant g**o**rilla.

grate, great
A **grate** is a framework of metal bars, and to **grate** means to shred.
Great means "very large" or "very good."

> the **grate** over the drain
> **grated** cheese
> a **great** expanse of water
> the **great** composers

grill, grille
A **grill** is a device for cooking food, and to **grill** food is to cook it on such
a device. A **grille** is a metal frame placed over an opening.

> Cook the chicken on the **grill**.
> **Grill** it for ten minutes.
> iron **grilles** over the windows

grisly, grizzly
Grisly means nasty and horrible. **Grizzly** means gray or streaked with
gray. A **grizzly** is also a type of bear.

> **grisly** murders
> a **grizzly** beard

hangar, hanger
A **hangar** is a place where airplanes are kept. A **hanger** is a shoulder-
shaped frame for storing clothes.

> a row of disused aircraft **hangars**
> Put your coat on a **hanger**.

hear, here
To **hear** is to become aware of a sound with your ears. Something that
is **here** is in, at or to this place or point.

> Can you **hear** me?
> We come **here** every summer.

heard, herd
Heard is the past tense of the verb **hear**. A *herd* is a group of animals that live, travel, or are grouped together.

> I **heard** that you were moving.
> We saw a **herd** of elk on the mountain this morning.

heir, air
An **heir** is someone who will inherit something. **Air** is the collection of gases that we breathe.

> His **heir** received a million dollars.
> polluted **air**

heroin, heroine
Heroin is a powerful illegal drug. The **heroine** of a story is the main female character in it.

> addicted to **heroin**
> the **heroine** of the film

hoard, horde
To **hoard** is to save things, and a **hoard** is a collection of things that have been saved. A **horde** is a large group of people, animals, or insects.

> a priceless **hoard** of modern paintings
> a **horde** of press photographers

hoarse, horse
Hoarse means "sounding rough or harsh." A **horse** is a large hoofed mammal.

> a **hoarse** voice
> a gallpoing **horse**

hour, our
An **hour** is a period of time. **Our** means "belonging to us."

> *a flight of four* **hours**
> **our** *favorite coffee shop*

humus, hummus
Humus is decaying vegetable material in the soil. **Hummus** is a food made from chickpeas.

> *soil enriched with* **humus**
> *a lunch of salad and* **hummus**

Hungary, hungry
Hungary is a European country. It is spelled with an **A**, unlike **hungry**, which means "wanting to eat."

> Remember: **Gary** from Hun**gary** gets an**gry** when he is hun**gry**.

idol, idle, idyll
An **idol** is a famous person worshipped by fans, or a picture or statue worshipped as a god. **Idle** means "doing nothing." An idyll is a poem or text about a peaceful, quiet setting.

> *The villagers worshipped golden* **idols**.
> *He's an* **idle** *bum.*
> *He composed* **idylls**, *ballads, and elegies.*

> Remember: To be id**le** takes **li**ttle **e**nergy.

it's, its

It's, with an apostrophe, is a shortened form of *it is*. **Its**, without an apostrophe, is used when you are referring to something belonging or relating to things that have already been mentioned.

> *It's cold.*
> *The lion lifted its head.*

kernel, colonel

A **kernel** is a seed or part of a nut. A **colonel** is an army officer.

> *apricot kernels*
> *a colonel in the French army*

> Remember: The co**lonel** is a **lonel**y man.

know, now

To **know** something means to be certain that it is true. **Now** means "at this moment."

> *Do you know the way to the bus station?*
> *I'm just leaving now.*

led, lead

Led is the past tense of the verb **lead**. **Lead**, when it is pronounced like **led**, is a soft metal, or the part of a pencil that makes a mark.

> *the road that led to the house*
> *lead poisoning*

liable, libel

Liable is an adjective meaning "responsible." It is related to **liability**. **Libel** is a noun and verb about publishing lies.

> *You will be liable for the cost.*
> *a case of libel*
> *She was libeled in the newspaper.*

lightening, lightning
Lightening is a form of the verb **lighten**, and means "becoming lighter." **Lightning**, without an **E**, is bright flashes of light in the sky.

> The sky was **lightening**.
> forked **lightning**

liquor, liqueur
Liquor is a general term for strong alcoholic drinks such as whiskey, gin, and vodka. A **liqueur** is a sweet, flavored alcoholic drink, usually drunk after a meal.

> a **liquor** store
> a selection of **liqueurs**

loath, loathe
If you are **loath** to do something, you are very unwilling to do it. To **loathe**, with an **E** at the end, is to hate something.

> I am **loath** to change it.
> I **loathe** ironing.

> Remember: I loath**e** that **E** at the end!

lose, loose
Something **loose** is not firmly held or not close-fitting. To **lose** something is not to have it any more, and to **lose** is also to be defeated.

> **loose** pants
> Why do you **lose** your temper?
> We win away games and **lose** home games.

martial, marshal
Martial is an adjective meaning "military." A **marshal** is a law enforcement officer.

martial law
A sky **marshal** on the flight made an arrest.

mat, matte
A **mat** is a covering for a floor. A **matte** color or surface has a dull appearance.

the kitchen **mat**
matte *photo paper*

medal, meddle
A **medal** is a round object given as a prize or award. To **meddle** means to interfere in an undesirable way.

the winner of four gold **medals**
Stop **meddling** *with my cell phone!*

metal, mettle
A **metal** is a hard substance such as iron or bronze. **Mettle** is your ability to deal with something difficult.

protective coverings made of **metal**
These debates will really test your **mettle**.

miner, minor
A **miner**, ending in **ER**, works in a mine. **Minor**, ending in **OR**, means "less important" or "less serious." A **minor** is also someone under eighteen.

His grandfather was a **miner**.
a **minor** *incident*

morning, mourning
The **morning** is the first part of the day. **Mourning** is a form of the verb **mourn**, and means "grieving for a dead person."

morning coffee
a period of *mourning* for the victims

mucus, mucous
Mucus is a slimy substance produced by the body. **Mucous** is an adjective meaning "relating to or producing mucus."

a discharge of *mucus*
mucous membranes

navel, naval
Your **navel** is the opening on your belly just above your waist. **Naval** is an adjective meaning "pertaining to or involving a navy."

of, off
Of is pronounced as if it ended with a **V** and is used in phrases like *a cup of tea* and *a friend of his*. **Off** is pronounced as it is spelled, and is the opposite of *on*.

a bunch *of* grapes
They stepped *off* the plane.
I turned the television *off*.

palate, palette, pallet
The **palate** is the top of the inside of the mouth, and your **palate** is also your ability to judge the taste of food and wine. A **palette** is a plate on which an artist mixes colors, and a **palette** is also a range of colors. A **pallet** is a platform on which items are stored or shipped.

a coffee to please every *palate*
a natural *palette* of earthy colors
crates of lettuce stacked on *pallets*

passed, past
Passed is the past tense of the verb **pass**. To go **past** something is to go beyond it. The **past** is the time before the present or describes things that existed before it.

*He had **passed** by the window.*
*I drove **past** without stopping.*
*the **past** few years*

peace, piece

Peace is a state of calm and quiet. A **piece** is a part of something.

*I enjoy the **peace** of the woods.*
*the missing **piece** of a jigsaw*

> Remember: a **pie**ce of **pie**.

pedal, peddle, petal

A **pedal** is a lever controlled with the foot, and to **pedal** something is to move its pedals. To **peddle** something is to sell it illegally. A **petal** is one of the outer colored parts of a flower.

***pedaling** her bicycle to work*
***peddling** drugs*
*perfume made from rose **petals***

pendant, pendent

A **pendant** is something you wear around your neck. **Pendent** is a less common word meaning "hanging."

*a **pendant** with a five-pointed star*
***pendent** yellow flowers*

personal, personnel

Personal means "belonging or relating to a person." **Personnel** are the people employed to do a job.

*a **personal** bodyguard*
*a change in **personnel***

pore, pour

If you **pore** over something, you study it carefully, and a **pore** is also a small hole in the surface of your skin. To **pour** something is to let it flow out of a container, and if something **pours**, it flows.

> *poring over a map*
> *The rain was **pouring** down.*

pray, prey

To **pray** means to say words to a god. An animal's **prey** is the thing it hunts and kills to eat.

> ***praying** for a good harvest*
> *a lion in search of its **prey***

precede, proceed

Something that **precedes** another thing happens before it. If you **proceed** you start or continue to do something.

> *This is explained in the **preceding** chapter.*
> *students who **proceed** to higher education*

prescribe, proscribe

To **prescribe** something is to recommend it. To **proscribe** something is to ban or forbid it.

> *The doctor will **prescribe** the right medicine.*
> *Two athletes were banned for taking **proscribed** drugs.*

principal, principle

Principal means "main" or "most important," and the **principal** of a school is the person in charge of it. A **principle** is a general rule, or a belief that you have about the way you should behave. **In principle** means "in theory."

> *The Festival has two **principal** themes.*
> *She is the **principal** of Pleasant View Elementary.*

*the basic **principles** of Marxism*
*The invitation had been accepted in **principle**.*

Remember: My **pal** is the princip**al**; you must l**ea**rn the princip**le**s.

prophecy, prophesy
Prophecy, with a **C**, is the noun. **Prophesy**, with an **S**, is the verb.

*I will never make another **prophecy**.*
*I **prophesy** that Norway will win.*

prophet, profit
A **prophet** is a spiritual leader who is thought to speak for a god. **Profit** is money earned from a business activity.

*the **prophet** Ezekiel*
***Profit** in the last quarter rose to $75 million.*

quiet, quite
Quiet means "not noisy." **Quite** means "fairly but not very."

*a **quiet** night in*
*He is **quite** shy.*

Remember: A qui**et** p**et** can have qu**ite** a b**ite**.

rain, reign, rein
Rain is water falling from the clouds. To **reign** is to rule a country or be the most noticeable feature of a situation. **Reins** are straps that control an animal, and to **rein in** something is to keep it under control.

*torrential **rain***
*She **reigned** for just nine days.*
*Peace **reigned** while Charlemagne lived.*
*Keep a tight grip on the **reins**.*
*She **reined** in her enthusiasm.*

road, rode
A **road** is a way leading from one place to another. **Rode** is the past tense of the verb **ride**.

> *a country* **road**
> *We* **rode** *in the back seat.*

roll, role
A **roll** is something with a round shape, and to **roll** something means to make it move like a ball. A **role** is the part that you play.

> *a* **roll** *of paper*
> *dinner* **rolls** *fresh from the oven*
> *to* **roll** *the dice*
> *He played a major* **role** *in the incident.*

skeptic, septic
A **skeptic** is a person who expresses doubts. Something that is **septic** is infected by bacteria.

> *a* **skeptic** *about religion*
> *The wound turned* **septic**.

> Remember that these words are both spelled the way they are pronounced.

sight, site, cite
Sight is the power to see, and a **sight** is something that you see. A **site** is a place with a special use. **Cite** means to refer to or mention as evidence of something.

> *an operation to improve his* **sight**
> *I can't stand the* **sight** *of all this mess.*
> *a building* **site**
> *The mayor* **cited** *several cases of misused funds.*

stationary, stationery

Stationary, with an **A**, means "not moving." **Stationery**, with an **E**, is paper, pens, and other writing equipment.

> *The traffic is **stationary**.*
> *the **stationery** cupboard*

> Remember: Station**e**ry is **e**nvelopes, but station**a**ry is st**a**nding still.

stile, style

A **stile** is a step that helps you climb over a wall or fence. **Style** is the way something is done, or an attractive way of doing things.

> *He clambered over the **stile**.*
> *cooked in genuine Chinese **style***
> *She dresses with such **style**.*

strait, straight

Strait means "narrow," and is found in the words *straitjacket* and *strait-laced*. A **strait** is a narrow strip of water. **Straight** means "not curved."

> *the **Straits** of Gibraltar*
> *a **straight** line*

symbol, cymbal

A **symbol** is something that represents another thing. A **cymbal** is a musical instrument.

> *a **symbol** of fertility*
> *the clash of the **cymbals***

team, teem
A **team** is a group of people engaged in a common effort. **Teem** is a verb meaning "overly full of."

> *a basketball **team***
> *a lake **teeming** with fish*

their, there, they're
Their is the spelling used to refer to something belonging or relating to people or things that have already been mentioned. **There** is the spelling for the word that says that something does or does not exist, draws attention to something, or says that something is at, in, or going to that place. **They're**, with an apostrophe, is a shortened form of *they are*.

> *people who bite **their** nails*
> ***There** is no life on Jupiter.*
> ***There**'s Kara!*
> *They didn't want me **there**.*
> ***They're** a good team.*

through, threw
Through means "going from one side to the other." **Threw** is the past tense of the verb *throw*.

> *They walked **through** the dense undergrowth.*
> *Youths **threw** stones at passing cars.*

tide, tied
The **tide** is the regular change in sea level. **Tied** is the past tense of the verb *tie*.

> *high **tide***
> *a beautifully **tied** bow*

two, to, too
Two is the number after one. The word **to** has many uses, such as indicating direction in phrases like *to the house* and forming the

infinitive of the verb, as in *to go*. **Too** means "in addition."

> *I have **two** sisters.*
> *We went **to** Barcelona.*
> *I need **to** leave soon.*
> *Will you come **too**?*

tongs, tongue

Tongs are instruments for holding and picking up things. Your **tongue** is the fleshy pink organ in your mouth.

> *curling **tongs***
> *It burned my **tongue**.*

vein, vain, vane

Vain means unsuccessful. **Vain** also means proud of your looks or abilities. **Veins** are tubes in your body through which your blood flows. A **vein** is also a mood or style. A weather **vane** is a device that shows wind direction.

> *a **vain** attempt to negotiate a truce*
> *You're so **vain**!*
> *the jugular **vein***

> Remember: To be **va**in is **v**ery **a**rrogant, but a **ve**in is a blood **ve**ssel. The weather va**ne** shows the wind coming from the **n**orth**e**ast.

waive, wave

To **waive** something is to give it up. A **wave** is a curled, moving body of water. To **wave** is also to move your hand in greeting or farewell.

> *The prisoner **waived** his right to a jury trial.*
> *Ten-foot **waves** washed onto the beach.*
> *Did you **wave** because you wanted me or just to say hi?*

waiver, waver

A **waiver** is an official document that allows an unusual action. To **waver** is to be undecided about something.

> *You must sign a **waiver** promising not to sue.*
> *I **wavered** over whether to cancel the meeting.*

wander, wonder

To **wander** is to walk around in a casual way. To **wonder** is to speculate or enquire about something.

> *She **wandered** aimlessly about the house.*
> *I **wonder** what happened*

way, weigh, whey

A **way** is a route or path, or a manner of doing something. To **weigh** something is to find out how heavy it is. **Whey** is the liquid part of milk that separates when you make cheese.

> *Is this the **way** to the beach?*
> *You're doing it the wrong **way**.*
> ***Weigh** the flour.*
> *curds and **whey***

weather, whether

The **weather** is the conditions in the atmosphere. **Whether** is a word used to introduce an alternative.

> *the **weather** forecast*
> *I'm not sure **whether** to stay or to go.*

wet, whet

Wet means "containing liquid" and to **wet** something means to add liquid. **Whet** is a verb that means "to sharpen" or "to make more intense."

*Your clothes are all **wet**.*
***Wet** the cloth and cover the bowl with it.*
*The smell of pie has **whetted** my appetite.*

which, witch
Which is a word used to introduce a question, or to refer to something or things that have already been mentioned. A **witch** is a woman with magical powers.

__Which__ house is it?
*The ring, **which** I had seen earlier, had now disappeared.*
*a story about **witches** and wizards*

whose, who's
Who's, with an apostrophe, is a shortened form of *who is*. **Whose**, without an apostrophe and with an **E** at the end, is used when you are asking who something belongs to, or referring to something belonging or relating to things that have already been mentioned.

*He knows **who's** boss.*
***Who's** there?*
*a little boy **whose** nose grew every time he told a lie*
***Whose** coat is this?*

wrap, rap
To **wrap** something means to put something around it, and a **wrap** is something that is folded around something else. A **rap** is a sharp blow, and **rap** is a style of music.

*to **wrap** presents*
*a turkey and cream cheese **wrap***
*a **rap** on the door*
*They like listening to **rap**.*

wring, ring
A **ring** is the sound made by a bell, and it is also a circle or enclosure.
To **wring** something is to twist it.

> the **ring** of the doorbell
> dancing in a **ring**
> **wringing** out the wet clothes

Remember: You **w**ring out something **w**et.

wry, rye
Wry means "mocking" or "ironic." **Rye** is a type of grass or grain.

> a **wry** smile
> a sandwich made with **rye** bread

yoke, yolk
A **yoke** is an oppressive force or burden. A **yoke** is also a wooden beam
put across two animals so that they can work together, and to **yoke**
things together is to link them. The yellow part of an egg is the **yolk**.

> a country under the **yoke** of oppression
> horses **yoked** to a plow
> I like the **yolk** to be runny.

your, you're, yore
Your, without an apostrophe, is used when you are referring to
something belonging or relating to the person or people you are
speaking to, or relating to people in general. **You're**, with an
apostrophe and with an **E** at the end, is a shortened form of *you are*.
Yore is a little-used word that occurs mainly in the phrase *days of yore*,
meaning "a time in the past."

> **Your** sister is right.
> Cigarettes can damage **your** health.
> **You're** annoying me.
> In days of **yore** I competed in marathons.

false
friends

False friends

Knowing that words are related to each other can be a great help to spelling. For example, when you spell *typical*, it can help to think of the related word *type* so that you know that the letter after the **T** is a **Y**.

But there are a few traps. Sometimes it seems logical that a word should follow a certain pattern or be spelled the same way as a word that sounds like it, but you will find that it doesn't. You will need to be alert when you spell the words listed here.

agoraphobia
> There is an **O** after the **G**. Don't be confused by *agriculture*.

ancillary
> There is no **I** after the **LL**. Don't be confused by *auxiliary*.

aqueduct
> There is no **A** after the **U**. Don't be confused by *aquarium*.

bachelor
> There is no **T** before the **CH**. Don't be confused by *batch*.

> Remember: Was **Bach** a **bach**elor?

comparison
> The letter after the **R** is an **I**. Don't be confused by *comparative*.

> Remember: There is no com**paris**on with **Paris**.

contemporary, temporary
> There words contain the sequence **TEMPOR**. Don't be confused by words like *temperature* and *temperament*.

curiosity
> There is no **U** after the **O**. Don't be confused by *curious*.

denunciation
> There is no **O** before the **U**. Don't be confused by *denounce*.

desperate, desperado
> The vowel after the **P** is **E**. Don't be confused by *despair*.

develop
There is no **E** on the end. Don't be confused by the ending of *envelope*.

disastrous
There is no **E** after the **T**. Don't be confused by *disaster*.

duly
There is no **E** after the **U**. Don't be confused by *due*.

extrovert
The vowel before the **V** is **O**. Don't be confused by *extra*.

flamboyant
There is no **U** before the **O**. Don't be confused by *buoyant*.

fiery
The sequence is **ER**, not **RE**. Don't be confused by *fire*.

forty
There is no **U** after the **O**. Don't be confused by *four*.

genealogy
The vowel before the **L** is **A**. Don't be confused by words like *geology*, *biology*, *ontology*, etc.

glamorous
There is no **U** after the first **O**. Don't be confused by *glamour*.

greyhound
It is spelled with an **E**, not an **A**. Don't be confused by the color *gray*.

hindrance
There is no **E** after the **D**. Don't be confused by *hinder*.

hypochondriac
The vowel after the **P** is **O**. Don't be confused by the more common prefix *hyper*.

inoculate
There is only one **N** after the **I**. Don't be confused by *innocuous*.

Israel
The vowel sequence is **AE**. Don't be confused by *real*.

kindergarten
The ending is **TEN**. Don't be confused by *garden*.

lavender
The vowel at the end is **E**. Don't be confused by *calendar*.

liquefy
The vowel before the **F** is **E**. Don't be confused by *liquid*.

minuscule

The vowel after the **N** is **U**. Don't be confused by *mini*, *minimum*, etc.

> Remember: This word is related to *minus*.

negligent

The vowel after the **L** is **I**. Don't be confused by *neglect*.

ninth

There is no **E** before the **TH**. Don't be confused by *nine*.

obscene

There is a **C** after the **S**. Don't be confused by *obsess*.

ostracize

The vowel in the middle is **A**. Don't be confused by *ostrich*.

personnel

There are two **N**'s. Don't be confused by *personal*.

primitive

The vowel after the **M** is **I**. Don't be confused by *primate*.

pronunciation

There is no **O** before the **U**. Don't be confused by *pronounce*.

questionnaire

There are two **N**'s. Don't be confused by *millionaire*.

refrigerator

There is no **D** before the **G**. Don't be confused by *fridge*.

sacrament

The middle vowel is **A**. Don't be confused by *sacred*.

sacrilegious

There is an **I** before the **L** and an **E** after the **L**. Don't be confused by *religion*.

supersede

The ending is **SEDE**. Don't be confused by words like *recede* and *precede*.

truly

There is no **E** after the **U**. Don't be confused by *true*.

veterinarian

There are **I**'s after both **R**'s. Don't be confused by *veteran*.

wondrous

There is no **E** after the **D**. Don't be confused by *wonder*.

other commonly misspelled words

Other commonly misspelled words

The final chapter of this book includes another list of words that are often spelled incorrectly. These words do not fall clearly under any of the categories covered in the previous five chapters.

Sometimes these words are hard to spell because the sound does not match the spelling. Sometimes the problem comes from the fact that a sound has several possible spellings and you need to know which applies in this particular word. Some of the words have unusual features about them.

It is worth familiarizing yourself with these words. Helpful ways of remembering the spelling have been provided for some of them.

absence
There is a single **S** at the beginning and a single **C** at the end – just the same as in its opposite, *presence*.
abysmal
The vowel sound after the **B** is spelled with a **Y**.
accede
The ending is **CEDE** – just the same as in *concede*, *precede*, and *recede*.
ache
The consonant sound is spelled **CH** and there is an **E** at the end.

> Remember: An **ache** needs **a che**ap remedy.

acknowledge
The second syllable is spelled **KNOW**.

> Remember: The word is made from *ac + knowledge*.

adequate
The vowel after the **D** is an **E**.
advantageous
There is an **E** after the **G**.

advertisement

There is an **E** after the **S**.

> Remember: The word is made up of *advertise* and the suffix **MENT**.

aerial

The beginning is **AE** – just the same as in *aerobic* and *aerosol*.

aesthetic

There is an **A** before the **E**. The spelling *esthetic* is sometimes used.

amethyst

The second vowel is **E** and the final vowel is **Y**.

analysis

The vowel after the **L** is **Y** and the final vowel is **I**.

annihilate

There are two **N**'s and the middle is **IHI** – just the same as in the related word *nihilism*.

anonymous

The vowel between the **N** and **M** is a **Y**, and the ending is **OUS**.

anxious

There is an **I** after the **X** – just as in *anxiety*.

apology

The vowel after the **L** is **O**.

> Remember: I will **log** an apo**log**y.

architect

There is an **H** after the **C**.

> Remember: The **arch** was designed by an **arch**itect.

argue

The ending is **UE**.

aspartame

The second vowel is **A**, just as in *asparagus*.

atheist

The first vowel is **A**, and the second vowel is **E**.

attendance

The ending is **ANCE**.

> Remember: You **dance** atten**dance** on someone.

atrocious

The ending is **CIOUS** – just the same as in *delicious*.

attach

There is no **T** before the **CH** – just the same as in the opposite word, *detach*.

> Remember: Atta**ch** a **c**oat **h**ook to the wall.

auxiliary

There is a single **L**, which is followed by an **I**.

awful

There is no **E** after the **W**, and a single **L** at the end.

bachelor

There is no **T** before the **CH**.

> Remember: Was **Bach** a **bach**elor?

barbecue

The correct spelling is **CUE**. The informal spelling is **Bar-B-Q**. Most people disapprove of the spelling *barbeque*.

because

The vowel sound after the **C** is spelled **AU**, and the ending is **SE**.

> Remember: **B**ig **e**lephants **c**an **a**lways **u**nderstand **s**mall **e**lephants.

beggar

The ending is **AR**.

> Remember: There is a beggar in the garden.

boundary

There is an **A** after the **D** that is sometimes not pronounced.

breadth

The vowel sound is spelled **EA** and there is a **D** before the **TH**.

Britain

The final vowel is spelled **AI** – just the same as in *certain*.

> Remember: There is a lot of rain in Britain.

broad

The vowel sound is spelled **OA**.

> Remember: Some roads can be quite broad.

bronchitis

There is an **H** after the **C**, and the ending is **ITIS**.

bruise

The ending is **UISE** – just the same as in *cruise*.

buoy

There is a **U** before the **O**.

> Remember: A buoy is a big unsinkable object yoked in the sea.

buoyant

There is a **U** before the **O** – just the same as in *buoy*.

bureaucracy

The vowel in the middle is spelled **EAU** and the ending is **CY**.

> Remember that the start of this word is the same as the word *bureau*.

burglar
The ending is **AR**.
business
The opening is **BUSI**.

Remember: It's none of your **busi**ness what **bus I** get!

caffeine
This is an exception to the rule "**I** before **E** except after **C**."
calendar
The vowel in the middle is **E** and the ending is **AR**.
carriage
There is an **I** before **AGE** – just the same as in *marriage*.
catalogue
The ending is **OGUE** – just the same as in *dialogue*. The spellings *catalog* and *dialog* are also used.
category
The vowel after the **T** is an **E**.
cauliflower
The first vowel is spelled **AU**.
ceiling
The word begins with a **C** and the first vowel sound is spelled **EI**.

Remember the rule: **I** before **E** *except after* **C**.

cellophane
The first letter is **C** and there is a **PH** in the middle.
cemetery
All of the vowels in this word are **E**'s.

Remember: A parking **meter** at the ce**meter**y.

certain
The final vowel is spelled **AI** – just the same as in *curtain*.

choir

Nothing much in this word looks like it sounds: the beginning is **CH** and the vowel sound is spelled **OIR**.

> Remember: **Cho**irs sing **cho**ral music.

claustrophobia

The first vowel sound is spelled **AU**, and there is an **O** before the **PH**.

cocoa

The first vowel is **O** and the second vowel sound is spelled **OA**.

coconut

There are two **O**'s – just the same as in *cocoa*.

coffee

There is a double **F** and the ending is **EE** – just the same as in *toffee*.

competent

The second and third vowels are both **E**.

> Remember: You must be **compete**nt in order to **compete**.

competition

The vowel after the **P** is an **E**.

> Remember: You **compete** in a **compet**ition.

complexion

The letter after the **E** is **X**.

concede

The ending is **CEDE** – just the same as in *accede*, *precede*, and *recede*.

conference

The vowel after the **F** is an **E** – just the same as in the related word *confer*.

congeal

The letter after the **N** is a **G**, and the ending is **EAL**.

conscience
> The sound after the first **N** is spelled **SCI**.

> Remember: The ending is the same as the word *science*.

conscientious
> The ending is **TIOUS**. The word is related to *conscience*, but the **C** changes to a **T**.

conscious
> The sound after the first **N** is spelled **SCI**.

continent
> The middle vowel is **I** and the ending is **ENT**.

controversial
> The vowel after the first **R** is an **O**.

convenient
> The ending is **ENT**.

counterfeit
> The ending is **EIT** – just the same as in *forfeit* and *surfeit*.

courteous
> The first vowel sound is spelled **OUR** and there is an **E** before the **OUS**.

criticize
> The letter after the second **I** is **C** – just the same as in the related word *critic*.

crocodile
> The middle vowel is an **O**.

> Remember: A cro**cod**ile has eaten a **cod**.

crucial
> The letter after the **U** is a **C**.

cruise
> The ending is **UISE** – just the same as in *bruise*.

other commonly misspelled words

currency
The vowel in the middle is an **E**.

curtain
The final vowel sound is spelled **AI** – just the same as in *certain*.

> Remember: Always buy pl**ain** curt**ain**s.

cyber-, cycle, cylinder, cynic, cyst
The beginning is **CY**.

decrease
The ending is **EASE** – just the same as in *increase*.

> Remember: Decr**ease** with **ease**.

definite
The vowel after the **F** is an **I**, and the ending is **ITE** – just the same as in the related word *finite*.

deliberate
The first vowel is **E**, and the ending is **ATE**.

> Remember the related word *deliberation*.

delicious
The ending is **CIOUS** – just the same as in *atrocious*.

describe
The first vowel is **E** – just the same as in *description*.

detach
There is no **T** before the **CH** – just the same as in the opposite word, *attach*.

deter
The ending is **ER**.

different
There is an **E** after the **F** that is sometimes not pronounced.

dilapidated
The beginning is **DI** (not **DE**).

> Remember: A **di**lapidated building is **di**sused.

dinosaur
The middle vowel is an **O**.

> Remember: There are **no** di**no**saurs **no**w.

eccentric
There are two **C**'s at the start.

ecstasy
The ending is **ASY** – just the same as in *fantasy*.

elegant
The vowel after the **L** is an **E**.

> Remember: E**leg**ant **leg**s.

eighth
There is only one **T**, even though the word comes from *eight* + the ending **TH**.

> Remember: **E**dith **is g**oing **h**ome **t**o Henry.

either
The **E** comes before the **I** – just the same as in the related word *neither*.

emphasis, emphasize
The sound after the **M** is spelled **PH**.

emphysema
The middle vowel is **Y**.

> Remember: You'll get emph**yse**ma if **y**ou **s**moke **e**nough.

encyclopedia
  The vowel before the **P** is an **O**.
endeavor
  The middle vowel sound is spelled **EA**.
exasperate
  The beginning is **EXA** and the vowel after the **P** is an **E**.
exercise
  The beginning is **EXE** and the ending is **ISE**.
expense
  The ending is **SE** – using an **S** as in the related word *expensive*.
extension
  The ending is **SION**.

> Remember that this word is related to *extensive*.

extravagant
  The vowel after the **V** is an **A**.

> Remember: There are an extravagant number of **A**'s in extr**a**v**a**g**a**nt.

facetious
  The ending is **TIOUS**.

> Remember: The word f**a**c**e**t**io**u**s** contains the vowels **AEIOU** in order.

family
  There is an **I** after the **M** that is sometimes not pronounced.

> Remember that you should be fam**i**liar with your fam**i**ly.

fascinate
  There is a **C** after the **S**.

fatigue
> The ending is **GUE**.

feasible
> The first vowel sound is spelled **EA** and the ending is **IBLE**.

February
> There is an **R** after the **B** that is often not pronounced.

feud
> The middle is spelled **EU**.

> Remember: **F**euds **e**nd **up d**isastrously.

fifth
> There is an **F** before the **TH**.

foreign
> The ending is **EIGN** – just the same as in *sovereign* and *reign*.
> This is an exception to the rule "**I** before **E** except after **C**."

forfeit
> The ending is **EIT** – just the same as in *counterfeit* and *surfeit*.
> This is an exception to the rule "**I** before **E** except after **C**."

friend
> There is an **I** before the **E**.

> Remember: **I** before **E**, except after **C**.

gauge
> There is a **U** after the **A**.

> Remember: **G**reat **A**unt **U**na **g**rows **e**ggplants.

generate, generation
> The vowel after the **N** is **E**.

genuine
> The ending is **INE**.

other commonly misspelled words

gipsy, gypsy
>The word can be spelled with either an **I** or a **Y** after the **G**.

glimpse
>There is a **P** before the **S** that is sometimes not pronounced.

grammar
>The ending is **AR**.

> Remember that gramm**ar** is related to gramm**a**tical.

gruesome
>There is an **E** after the **U** and another at the end.

guarantee, guard, guess, guide, guillotine, guilty, guitar
>There is a **U** after the **G** in these words.

gymnasium, gymnastics
>The vowel sound after the **G** is spelled with a **Y**.

gynecology
>The beginning is **GYN** – a sequence that occurs in some other words that pertain to women, such as *misogyny*.

harangue
>The ending is **GUE** – just the same as in *meringue* and *tongue*.

hatred
>The final vowel is **E**.

hearse
>The vowel sound is spelled **EA** and there is an **E** on the end.

> Remember: I didn't **hear** the **hear**se.

heifer
>The first vowel is spelled **EI** and there is only one **F**.

height
>The middle is **EIGH** – just the same as in *weight*.

heir
>There is a silent **H** and the ending is **EIR**.

> Remember: **H**appy **E**dward **i**s **r**ich.

holocaust
The vowel after the single **L** is an **O**.

horoscope
The vowel after the **R** is an **O**.

hyacinth
The vowel after the **H** is a **Y**, and the letter after the **A** is a **C**.

hygiene
The first vowel sound is a **Y** and the second vowel sound is spelled **IE**.

hyphen
The first vowel sound is a **Y**.

hypochondriac
The letter after the **P** is **O** and this is followed by **CH**.

hypocrite
The letter after the **P** is **O** and the ending is **ITE**.

hypocrisy
The letter after the **P** is **O** and the ending is **ISY**.

hysteria
The first vowel sound is a **Y**.

idiosyncrasy
The vowel after the **D** is **I**, the vowel after the first **S** is **Y**, and the ending is **ASY**.

incense
The letter after the first **N** is **C**, but the letter after the second **N** is **S**.

incident
The letter after the **N** is **C**, which is followed by an **I**.

incongruous
There is a **U** after the **R**.

increase
The ending is **EASE** – just the same as in *decrease*.

> Remember: Incr**eas**e with **ease**.

independent
The final vowel is an **E**.

input
>The opening is **IN**. This is an exception to the rule that the prefix **IN** changes to **IM** before a **P**.

integrate
>The vowel before the **G** is **E** – just the same as in *integral*.

intrigue
>The ending is **IGUE**.

introduce
>The vowel before the **D** is **O**.

irascible
>There is a **C** after the **S** and the ending is **IBLE**.

issue
>There is a double **S** in the middle – just the same as in *tissue*.

jealous, jealousy
>The first vowel sound is spelled **EA**; the second vowel is **OU** – just the same as in *zealous*.

journey
>The first vowel sound is spelled **OUR**.

Remember: How was y**our jour**ney?

judgment, judgement
>There is an optional **E** before the **M**, though most people prefer the shorter spelling.

knowledge
>The opening is **KNOW**.

Remember that **know**ledge is what you **know**.

knowledgeable
>There is an **E** after the **G**.

labyrinth
>The vowel sound after the **B** is a **Y**.

lackadaisical
There is a **CK** after the first **A** and the vowel sound after the **D** is spelled **AI**.

> Remember: If you **lack a dai**ly routine you are **lackadai**sical

lacquer
There is **CQU** in the middle.

language
The **U** comes before the **A**, which is the opposite of the way the letters fall in *gauge*.

languor
The ending is **UOR**.

> Remember: Liq**uor** may cause lang**uor**.

laugh
The vowel sound is spelled **AU** and the final consonant sound is spelled **GH**.

league
The ending is **GUE**.

lecherous
There is no **T** before the **CH**.

leisure
The **E** comes before the **I**.

length
There is a **G** after the **N** that is sometimes not pronounced.

liaise, liaison
There are two **I**'s in these words.

> Remember: **L**ouise **i**s **a**lways **i**n **s**ome **o**ld **n**ightgown.

licorice
The middle vowel is **O** and the ending is **ICE**.

> Remember: Have you ever tasted licor**ice ice** cream?

maintenance
The vowel after the **T** is an **E**, and the ending is **ANCE**.

> Remember: He does the main**tenan**ce for his **tenan**ts.

mantelpiece
The letters after the **T** are **EL**.

margarine
The vowel after the **G** is an **A**. This is an exception to the rule that **G** is "hard" before **A**, **O**, and **U**.

marriage
There is an **I** before **AGE** – just the same as in *carriage*.

massacre
There is a double **S** and the ending is **RE**.

> Remember: A **mass** of crops in every **acre**.

mathematics
There is an **E** after the **TH** that is sometimes not pronounced.

> Remember: I teach **them** mat**hem**atics.

messenger
The vowel after the **SS** is **E** – just the same as in *passenger*.

miscellaneous
There is a **C** after the first **S** and a double **L**.

> Remember: Mis**cell**aneous **cell**s.

misogyny
The ending is **GYNY**. The sequence **GYN** also occurs in some other words that pertain to women, such as *gynecology*.

money
The vowel after the **M** is **O**, and the ending is **EY**.

monkey
The vowel after the **M** is **O**, and the ending is **EY**.

mystery
The vowel sound after the **M** is **Y**, and the ending is **ERY**.

mystify
The vowel sound after the **M** is **Y** – just the same as in *mystery*.

nausea
The vowel after the **S** is **E**.

> Remember you might get nau**sea** at **sea**.

neither
The **E** comes before the **I** – just the same as in the related word *either*.

neural, neurotic, neutral
The opening is **NEU**.

niece
The **I** comes before the **E**, just as in *piece*.

nuisance
The opening is **NUI**.

onion
The first letter is **O**.

ophthalmologist, ophthalmology
The beginning is the unusual sequence **OPHTH** and there is an **L** before the **M** that is often not pronounced.

> Remember: O**phth**almologists **p**ractice **h**igh-**t**ech **h**ealing.

original
> The vowel after the **G** is an **I**.

> Remember: I orig**in**ally ordered **gin**.

ornament
> The vowel after the first **N** is an **A**.

oxygen
> The vowel after the **X** is a **Y** and the ending is **GEN** – just the same as in *hydrogen* and *nitrogen*.

pageant
> There is an **E** after the **G** that makes the **G** soft. There is no **D** before the **G**.

pamphlet
> There is a **PH** after the **M**.

parachute
> The ending is **CHUTE**.

particular
> There is an **AR** at the beginning and the end.

passenger
> The vowel after **SS** is **E** – just the same as in *messenger*.

peculiar
> The ending is **AR**.

penetrate
> The vowel after the **N** is **E**. *Perpetrate* has the same vowel pattern.

permanent
> The vowel after the **M** is an **A** and the vowel after the **N** is an **E**.

> Remember: A lion's **mane** is per**mane**nt.

persistent
> The ending is **ENT**.

persuade
> The beginning is **PER** and there is a **U** after the **S**.

phenomenon
The middle part is **NOM** and the ending is **NON**.

pigeon
There is an **E** before the **O** that makes the **G** soft. There is no **D** before the **G**.

pillar
There is a double **LL** and the ending is **AR**.

plagiarize
There is a **GI** in the middle.

Remember: The **GI** was guilty of pla**gi**arizing.

plague
The ending is **GUE**.

pneumonia
There is a silent **P** at the start and the first vowel sound is spelled **EU**.

Remember: **Pneu**monia **p**robably **n**ever **e**ases **u**p.

poignant
The **G** comes before the **N**.

prayer
The ending is **AYER**.

prejudice
The letter after **PRE** is **J**.

Remember: **Prej**udice is **prej**udging things.

prerogative
The beginning is **PRER**, not **PER** (which you might think from the way most people pronounce it).

prevalent
The vowel after the **V** is **A**.

privilege
>   The vowel after the **V** is **I** and the vowel after the **L** is **E**.

> Remember: It is **vile** to have no pri**vile**ges.

protein
>   This is an exception to the rule "**I** before **E** except after **C**."

provocation
>   The vowel after the **V** is **O**.

> Remember that this word is related to *provoke*.

pursue
>   There is an **R** after the first **U**.

pyramid
>   The first vowel is a **Y**.

quandary
>   There is an **A** after the **D** that is often not pronounced.

recede
>   The ending is **CEDE** – just the same as in *accede*, *concede*, and *precede*.

rehearsal
>   The vowel sound in the middle is spelled **EAR**.

> Remember: I **hear** there is a re**hear**sal.

reign
>   The ending is **EIGN** – just the same as in *sovereign* and *foreign*.

relevant
>   The vowel after the **L** is an **E**, and the vowel after the **V** is **A**.

religion
>   There is an **I** before the **O** and no **D** before the **G**.

reminisce
>   The vowel after the **M** is an **I**, and the ending is **ISCE**.

rhythm
> The beginning is **RH**, and the only vowel in this word is a **Y**.

> Remember: **R**hythm **h**elps **y**ou **t**o **h**ear **m**usic.

righteous
> The ending is **EOUS**.

rogue
> The ending is **OGUE** – just the same as in *vogue*.

rudimentary
> There is an **A** after the **T** that is often not pronounced.

sacrifice
> The vowel after the **R** is **I**. The ending is **ICE**.

sacrilege
> The vowel after the **L** is **E** – just the same as in *privilege*.

sausage
> The first vowel sound is spelled **AU**, and this is followed by a single **S**.

schedule
> The opening is **SCH**.

> Remember: The **sch**ool **sch**edule.

science, scientific
> The opening is **SC**.

scythe
> The opening is **SC**, the main vowel is **Y**, and there is an **E** at the end.

secretary
> The vowel before the **T** is **E**.

> Remember: The **secret**ary can keep a **secret**.

seize
> This is an exception to the rule "**I** before **E** except after **C**."

separate
>   The vowel after the **P** is **A**.

>   Remember that this word has the word *par* contained inside it.

sergeant
>   The first vowel sound is spelled **ER**, and this is followed by **GE**.

series
>   The ending is **IES**.

serious
>   The ending is **OUS**.

several
>   There is an **E** after the **V** that is sometimes not pronounced.

shoulder
>   There is a **U** after the **O**.

sieve
>   There is an **E** after the **I**, and another **E** at the end.

>   Remember: A **sieve** is for **si**fting **eve**rything.

similar
>   There is an **I** after the **M** that is not fully pronounced, and the ending is **AR**.

>   Remember: A **simil**e compares things that are **simil**ar.

simultaneous
>   There is an **E** after the **N**.

skeleton
>   The vowel after the **L** is **E**.

>   Remember: Don't **let on** about the ske**leton** in the closet.

somersault

The first vowel is an **O**, and the final vowel sound is spelled **AU**.

soothe

There is an **E** at the end.

sovereign

The ending is **EIGN** – just the same as in *foreign* and *reign*.

> Remember: A sove**reign reign**s.

spontaneous

There is an **E** after the second **N**.

stealth, stealthy

There is an **A** after the **E** – just the same as in *wealth* and *wealthy*.

stereo

The vowel after the **R** is an **E**.

> Remember: St**ere**o **re**cords.

stomach

The first vowel is an **O**, and the ending is **ACH**.

strength

There is a **G** after the **N** that is sometimes not pronounced.

surfeit

The ending is **EIT** – just the same as in *counterfeit* and *forfeit*.

surgeon

There is an **E** between the **G** and the **O**.

> Remember: Surg**eo**ns give **e**ffective **o**perations.

surprise

There is an **R** before the **P**.

susceptible

There is a **C** after the second **S**. The ending is **IBLE**.

sustenance

The vowel after the **T** is **E**.

synonym
There is a **Y** after the **S** and one before the **M**.

syringe
There is a **Y** after the **S**. The ending is **GE**.

tacit
The middle consonant is a **C**.

temperament, temperature
There is an **A** after the **R** that is often not pronounced.

thorough
The final vowel sound is spelled **OUGH**.

through
The vowel sound is spelled **OUGH**.

tissue
There is a double **S** in the middle – just the same as in *issue*.

toffee
There is a double **F** and the ending is **EE** – just the same as in *coffee*.

tongue
The ending is **GUE** – just the same as in *harangue*.

tragedy
There is no **D** before the **G**.

> Remember: I **raged** at the **traged**y of it.

twelfth
There is an **F** before the **TH** that is often not pronounced.

typical
The letter after the **T** is a **Y** – just the same as in *type*.

usual
The letter after the first **U** is **S**.

> Remember: **U**gly **s**wan **u**ses **a** **l**ipstick.

vaccinate
There is double **C** – just the same as in *access* and *accent*.

vague

> The ending is **AGUE**.

varicose

> The first vowel is **A**.

vegetable

> The vowel after the **G** is an **E**.

> Remember: **Get** some ve**get**ables inside you!

vehement

> There is an **H** after the first **E** that is often not pronounced.

vogue

> The ending is **OGUE** – just the same as in *rogue*.

weird

> This is an exception to the rule "**I** before **E** except after **C**."

worship

> The vowel sound is spelled **OR**.

wrath

> There is a silent **W**, and the vowel is an **A**.

yacht

> This is a very unusual spelling: the middle part of the word is **ACH**.

zealous

> The first vowel sound is spelled **EA**; the second vowel is **OU** – just the same as in *jealous*.

> Remember that this word is related to *zeal*.

index
of hard
words